Uncover 2 Combo A

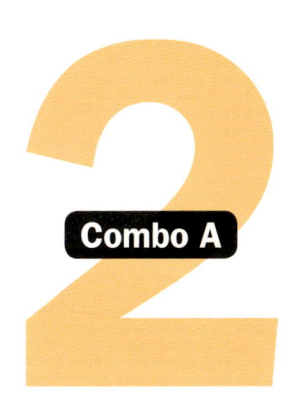

Ben Goldstein • Ceri Jones
with Kathryn O'Dell

Student's Book

CAMBRIDGE UNIVERSITY PRESS

Discovery EDUCATION

CAMBRIDGE
UNIVERSITY PRESS

University Printing House, Cambridge CB2 8BS, United Kingdom

One Liberty Plaza, 20th Floor, New York, NY 10006, USA

477 Williamstown Road, Port Melbourne, VIC 3207, Australia

314–321, 3rd Floor, Plot 3, Splendor Forum, Jasola District Centre,
New Delhi – 110025, India

79 Anson Road, #06-04/06, Singapore 079906

Cambridge University Press is part of the University of Cambridge.

It furthers the University's mission by disseminating knowledge in the pursuit of
education, learning and research at the highest international levels of excellence.

www.cambridge.org
Information on this title: www.cambridge.org/9781107515055

© Cambridge University Press 2015

This publication is in copyright. Subject to statutory exception
and to the provisions of relevant collective licensing agreements,
no reproduction of any part may take place without the written
permission of Cambridge University Press.

First published 2015

20 19 18 17 16 15 14

Printed in Poland by Opolgraf

A catalog record for this publication is available from the British Library

ISBN 978-1-107-49320-9 Student's Book 2
ISBN 978-1-107-49323-0 Student's Book with Online Workbook and Online Practice 2
ISBN 978-1-107-51505-5 Combo 2A
ISBN 978-1-107-51506-2 Combo 2B
ISBN 978-1-107-49331-5 Teacher's Book 2
ISBN 978-1-107-49328-5 Workbook with Online Practice 2
ISBN 978-1-107-49338-4 Presentation Plus Disc 2
ISBN 978-1-107-49333-9 Class Audio CDs 2
ISBN 978-1-107-49335-3 DVD 2

Additional resources for this publication at www.cambridge.org/uncover

The publishers have no responsibility for the persistence or accuracy of URLs
for external or third-party Internet websites referred to in this publication, and
do not guarantee that any content on such websites is, or will remain, accurate
or appropriate. Information regarding prices, travel timetables, and other factual
information given in this work is correct at the time of first printing but the
publishers do not guarantee the accuracy of such information thereafter.

Art direction, book design, layout services, and photo research: QBS Learning
Audio production: John Marshall Media

Acknowledgments

Many teachers, coordinators, and educators shared their opinions, their ideas, and their experience to help create *Uncover*. The authors and publisher would like to thank the following people and their schools for their help in shaping the series.

In Mexico:
María Nieves Maldonado Ortiz (Colegio Enrique Rébsamen); Héctor Guzmán Pineda (Liceo Europeo); Alfredo Salas López (Campus Universitario Siglo XXI); Rosalba Millán Martínez (IIPAC [Instituto Torres Quintero A.C.]); Alejandra Rubí Reyes Badillo (ISAS [Instituto San Angel del Sur]); José Enrique Gutiérrez Escalante (Centro Escolar Zama); Gabriela Juárez Hernández (Instituto de Estudios Básicos Amado Nervo); Patricia Morelos Alonso (Instituto Cultural Ingles, S.C.); Martha Patricia Arzate Fernández, (Colegio Valladolid); Teresa González, Eva Marina Sánchez Vega (Colegio Salesiano); María Dolores León Ramírez de Arellano, (Liceo Emperadores Aztecas); Esperanza Medina Cruz (Centro Educativo Francisco Larroyo); Nubia Nelly Martínez García (Salesiano Domingo Savio); Diana Gabriela González Benítez (Colegio Ghandi); Juan Carlos Luna Olmedo (Centro Escolar Zama); Dulce María Pascual Granados (Esc. Juan Palomo Martínez); Roberto González, Fernanda Audirac (Real Life English Center); Rocio Licea (Escuela Fundación Mier y Pesado); Diana Pombo (Great Union Institute); Jacobo Cortés Vázquez (Instituto María P. de Alvarado); Michael John Pryor (Colegio Salesiano Anáhuac Chapalita)

In Brazil:
Renata Condi de Souza (Colégio Rio Branco); Sônia Maria Bernal Leites (Colégio Rio Branco); Élcio Souza (Centro Universitário Anhaguera de São Paulo); Patricia Helena Nero (Private teacher); Célia Elisa Alves de Magalhães (Colégio Cruzeiro-Jacarepaguá); Lilia Beatriz Freitas Gussem (Escola Parque-Gávea); Sandra Maki Kuchiki (Easy Way Idiomas); Lucia Maria Abrão Pereira Lima (Colégio Santa Cruz-São Paulo); Deborah de Castro Ferroz de Lima Pinto (Mundinho Segmento); Clara Vianna Prado (Private teacher); Ligia Maria Fernandes Diniz (Escola Internacional de Alphaville); Penha Aparecida Gaspar Rodrigues (Colégio Salesiano Santa Teresinha); Silvia Castelan (Colégio Santa Catarina de Sena); Marcelo D'Elia (The Kids Club Guarulhos); Malyina Kazue Ono Leal (Colégio Bandeirantes); Nelma de Mattos Santana Alves (Private teacher); Mariana Martins Machado (Britannia Cultural); Lilian Bluvol Vaisman (Curso Oxford); Marcelle Belfort Duarte (Cultura Inglesa-Duque de Caxias); Paulo Dantas (Britannia International English); Anauã Carmo Vilhena (York Language Institute); Michele Amorim Estellita (Lemec – Lassance Modern English Course); Aida Setton (Colégio Uirapuru); Maria Lucia Zaorob (CEL-LEP); Marisa Veiga Lobato (Interlíngua Idiomas); Maria Virgínia Lebrón (Independent consultant); Maria Luiza Carmo (Colégio Guilherme Dumont Villares/CEL-LEP); Lucia Lima (Independent consultant); Malyina Kazue Ono Leal (Colégio Bandeirantes); Debora Schisler (Seven Idiomas); Helena Nagano (Cultura Inglesa); Alessandra de Campos (Alumni); Maria Lúcia Sciamarelli (Colégio Divina Providência); Catarina Kruppa (Cultura Inglesa); Roberto Costa (Freelance teacher/consultant); Patricia McKay Aronis (CEL-LEP); Claudia Beatriz Cavalieri (By the World Idiomas); Sérgio Lima (Vermont English School); Rita Miranda (IBI – [Instituto Batista de Idiomas]); Maria de Fátima Galery (Britain English School); Marlene Almeida (Teacher Trainer Consultant); Flávia Samarane (Colégio Logosófico); Maria Tereza Vianna (Greenwich Schools); Daniele Brauer (Cultura Inglesa/AMS Idiomas); Allessandra Cierno (Colégio Santa Dorotira); Helga Silva Nelken (Greenwich Schools/Colégio Edna Roriz); Regina Marta Bazzoni (Britain English School); Adriano Reis (Greenwich Schools); Vanessa Silva Freire de Andrade (Private teacher); Nilvane Guimarães (Colégio Santo Agostinho)

In Ecuador:
Santiago Proaño (Independent teacher trainer); Tania Abad (UDLA [Universidad de Las Americas]); Rosario Llerena (Colegio Isaac Newton); Paúl Viteri (Colegio Andino); Diego Maldonado (Central University); Verónica Vera (Colegio Tomás Moro); Mónica Sarauz (Colegio San Gabriel); Carolina Flores (Colegio APCH); Boris Cadena, Vinicio Reyes (Colegio Benalcázar); Deigo Ponce (Colegio Gonzaga); Byron Freire (Colegio Nuestra Señora del Rosario)

The authors and publisher would also like to thank the following contributors, script writers, and collaborators for their inspired work in creating *Uncover*:
Anna Whitcher, Janet Gokay, Kathryn O'Dell, Lynne Robertson, and Dana Henricks

Unit	Vocabulary	Grammar	Listening	Conversation (Useful language)
1 Traditions pp. 2–11	■ Categories ■ Clothes and objects	■ Simple present review with *be* and *have* ■ *whose* and possessives Grammar reference p. 106	■ Whose shoes are they?	■ Keeping a conversation going
2 What's Playing? pp. 12–21	■ Types of movies ■ Types of TV shows	■ Simple present review ■ Adverbs of frequency ■ Verb + infinitive or *-ing* form (gerund) Grammar reference p. 107	■ Deciding what to watch	■ Asking for and giving opinions
3 Spending Habits pp. 22–31	■ Places to shop ■ Money verbs	■ Present continuous review ■ Simple present vs. present continuous ■ Quantifiers Grammar reference p. 108	■ Shopping habits	■ Making requests when shopping
4 Our Heroes pp. 32–41	■ Cool jobs ■ Adjectives of personality	■ Simple past statements review and *ago* ■ Simple past questions review and *ago* Grammar reference p. 109	■ Interview with a teenage hero	■ Asking for and giving clarification
5 It's a Mystery! pp. 42–51	■ Action verbs ■ Adverbs of manner	■ Past continuous ■ Adverbs of time ■ Simple past vs. past continuous ■ *when* and *while* Grammar reference p. 110	■ I saw something strange last night.	■ Telling and reacting to a story

Units 1–5 Review Game pp. 52–53

Writing	Reading	Video	Accuracy and fluency	Speaking outcomes
A description of a family tradition	*At Home in Two Worlds* Reading to write: *Our Summer Tradition* Culture: *Colorful Hands and Heads*	*Carpets of Dagestan* *What's your favorite place in town?* *A Very Indian Wedding*	*whose* vs. *who's* Pronouncing the possessive of names ending in *-s*	I can . . . identify and talk about modern and traditional things talk about modern and traditional things in my life ask and answer questions about possessions keep a conversation going talk about sports, weddings, and other traditions
A movie review	*Cinema's Best Villains* Reading to write: *My All-Time Favorite Movie* Culture: *Hooray for Bollywood!*	*A Life on Broadway* *What types of TV shows do you like watching?* *Mumbai: From Computers to Film* *Who's Real?* (CLIL Project p. 116)	Infinitive or *-ing* form (gerund) vs. base form after some verbs Irregular spellings of third person simple present form The /ʃ/ sound	I can . . . identify different types of movies talk about my movie-watching habits talk about different types of TV shows, preferences, and TV habits ask for and give opinions compare Hollywood movies with other movies
A product review	*A Day at the Mall in Dubai* Reading to write: *Product Reviews* Culture: *Adopt an Animal*	*Unusual Fun* *How do you spend your money?* *Zero: Past and Present*	*enough* and *not enough* Irregular spellings of the *-ing* form syllable stress in compound nouns	I can . . . identify places to shop talk about the things I do every day and the things I'm doing now ask and answer questions about spending and saving money make requests when shopping talk about using money to help people or animals
A description of a person you admire	*Young and Talented!* Reading to write: *My Hero* Culture: *The Island of Champions*	*Wildlife Hero* *Who is your role model and why?* *The Chilean Mine Rescue* *Amelia Earhart: Famous Flyer* (CLIL Project p. 117)	Irregular verbs in the simple past Spelling rules for the simple past Short and long *i* sounds	I can . . . identify some cool jobs share facts about someone's life ask and answer questions about being brave ask for and give clarification talk about famous athletes from my country
A narrative about an interesting or unusual event	*Whodunit?* Reading to write: *An Urban Legend* Culture: *The World's Number One Detective*	*Mysteries in the Mountains* *What's an unusual or interesting thing that happened to you recently?* *The Case of the Missing Woman* *An Underwater Mystery* (CLIL Project p. 118)	The simple past for an event that interrupts an event in progress Spelling rules for forming adverbs Pronouncing *was*	I can . . . tell a story with action verbs talk about what I was doing in the past talk about past events and describe how I do things tell an interesting or unusual story understand information and talk about fictional characters

1 Traditions

Discovery EDUCATION
BE CURIOUS

- Carpets of Dagestan
- What's your favorite place in town?
- A Very Indian Wedding

1. Where are the women?

2. What are they like? How are they different from other people in the photo?

3. Do you ever wear traditional clothes? When?

UNIT CONTENTS
Vocabulary Categories; clothes and objects
Grammar Simple present review with *be* and *have*; *whose* and possessives
Listening Whose shoes are they?

Vocabulary: Categories

1. Label the sets of traditional and modern pictures with the correct words.

art   clothing   food   ✓music   places   sports

1. _music_   2. _____

3. _____   4. _____

5. _____   6. _____

NOTICE IT
Another word for **clothing** is **clothes**. **Clothing** is usually used for the general category. **Clothes** is usually used for specific items.
There are two clothing stores in the mall.
I need some new clothes.

2. Listen, check, and repeat.

3. Do the pictures in Exercise 1 show modern or traditional things? Check (✓) the correct answers.

Photo	a	b	c	d	e	f	g	h	i	j	k	l
Traditional	✓											
Modern		✓										

Speaking: Likes and dislikes

4. **YOUR TURN** Work with a partner. Do you like traditional or modern things for the categories in Exercise 1? Can you name any traditional and modern things for each category?

> I like modern music. Hip-hop is modern. I don't like traditional music. Jazz is traditional.

> I like traditional and modern sports. Sumo wrestling is traditional. Basketball is modern.

▶ Workbook, p. 2

Reading At Home in Two Worlds; Our Summer Tradition; Colorful Hands and Heads
Conversation Keeping a conversation going
Writing A description of a family tradition

Unit 1 | 3

OLD and NEW

At Home in Two Worlds

Meet Maria! She is 14, and she lives in Otavalo, Ecuador. She has a traditional and a modern life. She lives in a modern house with her family. Maria has a brother. He's 17. She also has a sister. She's 12. Maria and her family make traditional art, and they sell it at a big market in Otavalo. They sell their art online, too. Maria's brother and father are also musicians, and they play traditional music. Maria likes traditional music, but she also listens to modern rock music at home.

Maria doesn't have modern clothes. She wears traditional clothes and jewelry. She eats traditional food with her family. She has meat with corn, potatoes, or beans. After school, she sometimes eats in modern restaurants with her friends. Maria speaks Quechua, an ancient Incan language, with her parents. She speaks Spanish with her brother, sister, and friends. She and her sister also have English classes at school. Maria likes her traditional and modern life!

DID YOU KNOW…?
The market in Otavalo has clothing, art, and food. It's popular with people from Ecuador and from around the world.

Reading: An article about life in Otavalo, Ecuador

1. Look at the photos. Is the family modern or traditional?

2. Read and listen to the article. Who is in Maria's family? What do they do?

3. Read the article again. Check (✓) the things that are true for Maria. Sometimes both answers are possible.

   1. ☐ lives in a traditional house   ☐ lives in a modern house
   2. ☐ has a younger sister   ☐ has an older sister
   3. ☐ has one brother   ☐ has two brothers
   4. ☐ listens to traditional music   ☐ listens to modern music
   5. ☐ wears traditional clothes   ☐ wears modern clothes
   6. ☐ eats traditional food   ☐ eats modern food

4. **YOUR TURN** Work with a partner. How are you like Maria? How are you different?

   > Maria is 14, and I'm . . .

Grammar: Simple present review with be and have

5. Complete the chart.

Use the simple present of be to identify people and give locations and dates.
Use the simple present of have to talk about possessions, characteristics, and relationships.

be	have
Wh- questions and answers	
Where **are** you? **I'm** in Otavalo. **I'm** _____ in Quito.	When **do** you _____ art class? I **have** art at 10:00. I **don't have** art at 9:00.
How old _____ she? **She's** 14. She **isn't** 17.	What **does** she **have** for dinner? She _____ meat. She **doesn't have** fish.
Who **are** they? They _____ Maria's parents. They **aren't** her grandparents.	What **do** they **have**? They **have** a computer. They _____ a desk.
Yes/No questions and answers	
_____ you in Otavalo? Yes, I **am**. / No, **I'm not**.	**Do** you **have** art at 10:00? Yes, I _____. / No, I **don't**.
Is she 14? Yes, she _____. / No, she **isn't**.	_____ she **have** meat for dinner? Yes, she **does**. / No, she **doesn't**.
Are they Maria's parents? Yes, they **are**. / No, they _____.	Do they **have** a computer? Yes, they **do**. / No, they _____.

> Check your answers: Grammar reference, p. 106

6. Match the questions with the answers.

1. Is your brother tall? _c_
2. Are they from Ecuador? ___
3. Where are you? ___
4. How many sisters do you have? ___
5. Does Jake have a truck? ___

a. I have three.
b. I'm in my English class.
c. No, he's not.
d. No, he doesn't.
e. Yes, they are.

7. Complete the conversations with the correct form of be or have.

1. **A:** When _____ your music class?
   B: It _____ on Monday.
2. **A:** _____ Kate and Dennis _____ a truck?
   B: Yes, they _____. They _____ two trucks.
3. **A:** _____ your parents home?
   B: No, they _____. They _____ at work right now.
4. **A:** _____ your house small?
   B: No, it _____. It _____ big.

Speaking: My life

8. YOUR TURN Work with a partner. Tell your partner about something modern and something traditional in your life.

> I have a traditional house. It's very old. My clothes are modern. They . . .

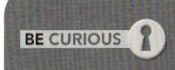

BE CURIOUS Find out about carpet makers in Russia. What is life like in Dagestan? (Workbook, p. 72)

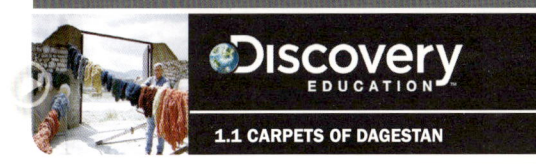

Discovery EDUCATION
1.1 CARPETS OF DAGESTAN

MY Things

Listening: Whose shoes are they?

1. Do your parents or grandparents have things from the past? What do they have?

2. Listen to Wendy and Josh talk about old things in their grandparents' house. Check (✓) the people the things belong to.

   ☐ father   ☐ grandfather   ☐ great-grandfather
   ☐ mother   ☐ grandmother   ☐ great-grandmother

3. Listen again. Circle the adjectives that describe the things Wendy and Josh find. There is more than one answer for each item.

   1. First object: **big / small / heavy / colorful / slow**
   2. Second object: **new / old / cool / old-fashioned**
   3. Third object: **white / black / big / small**

Vocabulary: Clothes and objects

4. Match the words with the correct pictures. Then listen and check your answers.

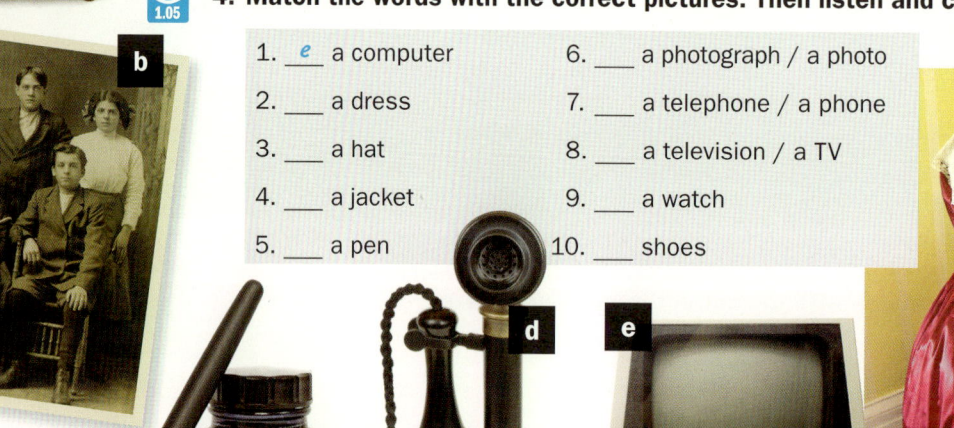

   1. _e_ a computer
   2. ___ a dress
   3. ___ a hat
   4. ___ a jacket
   5. ___ a pen
   6. ___ a photograph / a photo
   7. ___ a telephone / a phone
   8. ___ a television / a TV
   9. ___ a watch
   10. ___ shoes

5. **YOUR TURN** Work with a partner. What are the items in Exercise 4 like today?

   > TVs are big today, and they have flat screens. TV shows are in color.

Grammar: *whose* and possessives

6. Complete the chart.

Use *whose* to ask about possession.
Use a name/noun + 's, a possessive adjective, or a possessive pronoun to show possession.

Whose	_____ computer is it? / **Whose** is it?
	Whose shoes are they? / **Whose** are they?
Possessive 's or s'	It's Dad**'s** computer.
	They're our grandmother_____ shoes.
	That's our grandparent**s'** house.
Possessive adjectives	It's **his** computer.	my your
	They're **her** shoes.	_____ her its
	That's **their** house.	our _____
Possessive pronouns	It's **his**.	mine yours
	They're **hers**.	his _____ its
	That's **theirs**.	ours _____

> Check your answers: Grammar reference, p. 106

7. Write questions and answers for the information in the chart. Use possessive 's and s' for the answers.

	Doug	Sofia	my cousins
1. hat		✓	
2. TV			✓
3. pens	✓		

1. *Whose hat is it? It's Sofia's hat.*
2. _____
3. _____

Get it RIGHT!

Do not confuse *whose* with *who's*:
who's = *who is*.
Whose phone is this?
NOT: ~~**Who's** phone is this?~~

8. Rewrite the sentences two ways. Use possessive adjectives and possessive pronouns.

1. It's my sisters' soccer ball.   *It's their soccer ball. It's theirs.*
2. They're Jack's paintings.   _____
3. It's my aunt's jacket.   _____

Speaking: Whose is it?

9. YOUR TURN Work with a small group. Each person puts two small items in a bag. The others don't look. Take out an item and have the others guess whose it is. Take turns.

Say it RIGHT!

If a name ends in -s, add 's after the final -s. You can also just use an apostrophe (') after the final -s. Both are correct, and they are pronounced the same way. For example, *Lucas's* and *Lucas'* both sound like *Lucases*. Listen to the sentences.
  Lucas has hats. = They're Luca**s's** hats. / They're Luca**s'** hats.
Pay attention to the way you pronounce your classmates' names with the possessive in Exercise 9.

> Workbook, pp. 4–5

REAL TALK 1.2 WHAT'S YOUR FAVORITE PLACE IN TOWN?

New TRADITIONS

Conversation: A cool tradition

1. **REAL TALK** Watch or listen to the teenagers. Check (✓) their favorite places.

☐ a bedroom	☐ a gym	☐ a restaurant	☐ an ice cream shop
☐ a computer lab	☐ a library	☐ a stadium	☐ a movie theater
☐ a park	☐ a mall	☐ a supermarket	

2. **YOUR TURN** What's *your* favorite place in town? Tell your partner.

3. Listen to Tom telling Eva about a family tradition. Complete the conversation.

   USEFUL LANGUAGE: Keeping a conversation going
   Tell me about it.   That's interesting.   Really?   Then what?

   Eva: Hey, what's that?
   Tom: It's my **grandfather's** old **watch**. Well, now it's my **watch**!
   Eva: 1 _____
   Tom: Yeah. We have this cool tradition for my **grandfather's** birthday.
   Eva: 2 _____
   Tom: Well, we always have a party **in the park**. It's **his** favorite place. We eat traditional food. We have **burgers** and, of course, birthday cake.
   Eva: 3 _____
   Tom: Well, we never give gifts to my **grandfather**. After we eat, **he** gives *us* gifts.
   Eva: 4 _____ Why does he do that?
   Tom: He wants us to have his things. So, now I have **his** cool **watch**!

4. Practice the conversation with a partner.

5. **YOUR TURN** Repeat the conversation in Exercise 3, but change the words in purple. Use the information in the chart for one conversation and your own ideas for another.

		My ideas
Person	aunt	
Item	scarf	
Place	in a restaurant	
Food	tacos	

8 | Unit 1

Our Summer Tradition

by Carla Lucero

I have a big Italian family, and we have an unusual tradition. On the last day of school, we always have dinner at an Italian restaurant. We celebrate the start of summer! There are always a lot of people at the restaurant — my parents, my grandparents, my brother, my sister, my cousins, and me!

We have traditional Italian food. There are many great dishes on the menu, like minestrone soup and pasta. We also have dessert. There is traditional Italian music at the restaurant, too. After dinner, we go to my grandparents' house and watch an Italian movie. Then we look at family photos. It's really fun.

Reading to write: A family tradition

6. **Look at the photo. Where are the people? Who do you think they are? Read the article to check.**

> ● *Focus on* **CONTENT**
> When you write about a tradition, include this information:
> - what
> - why
> - when
> - who
> - where

7. **Read Carla's article again. Find examples for the categories in the Focus on Content box.**

> ● *Focus on* **LANGUAGE**
> **there is / there are**
> Use **there is / there are** to give information about what, when, where, why, and who in a description of something, such as a family tradition.
> - **There is** a big table in the restaurant.
> - **There are** many musicians at our summer picnic.

8. **Find examples of *There is / There are* in Carla's article.**

9. **Complete the sentence with *There is* or *There are*.**

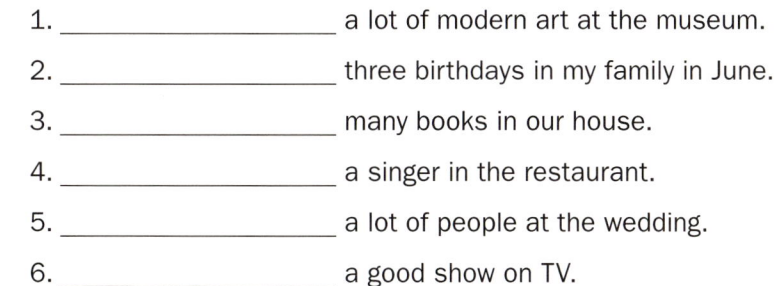

   1. _____ a lot of modern art at the museum.
   2. _____ three birthdays in my family in June.
   3. _____ many books in our house.
   4. _____ a singer in the restaurant.
   5. _____ a lot of people at the wedding.
   6. _____ a good show on TV.

Writing: My family tradition

◻ **PLAN**
Choose a tradition in your family. Make a word web with the topics from the Focus on Content box.

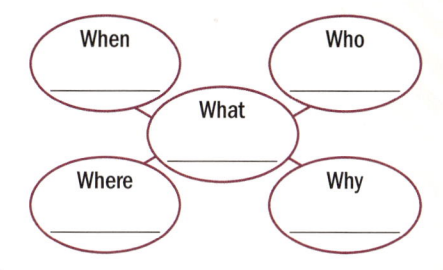

(Word web with: When, Who, What, Where, Why)

◻ **WRITE**
Now write about the tradition. Use your notes to help you. Write at least 60 words.

◻ **CHECK**
Check your writing. Can you answer "yes" to these questions?

- Is information for each category from the Focus on Content box in your article?
- Do you use *there is* and *there are* correctly?

COLORFUL HANDS AND HEADS

What color is your hair? In many cultures, people change their hair color for some traditions. Face and body painting is a tradition in many places, too. These traditions are new and old!

The Romanian soccer team at the World Cup
Citrus College fans at a soccer game

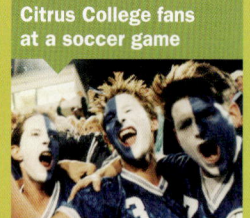

_____
Some sports teams color their hair with their team colors. For example, a high school swim team has blue hair for a swimming event. A professional soccer team has yellow hair for the World Cup. Sports fans often paint their faces with school colors, too. At many sports events, there are people in school colors from head to toe!

A wedding in, India

_____
In some traditional weddings in India, the bride has designs on her hands with henna, a special paint. During the wedding, the groom colors the middle of the bride's hair red. It is a symbol of marriage.

A teenager in the Omo Valley

_____
It is hot and sunny in the Omo Valley in Africa. Mursi and Surma people paint their faces, heads, and bodies with clay from the earth. It protects them from the sun. It is a tradition, and it is also art. They have white, yellow, red, and gray designs on their faces and bodies. They have colorful clay in their hair, too, and sometimes they make and wear interesting hats.

New or old, hair coloring and face painting are interesting traditions!

Culture: Hair coloring and face painting traditions

1. Look at the photos. Where are the people? What colors do you see?

2. Read the article. Complete the text with the headings. Then listen and check your answers.

   Tradition and Art   A New Sports Tradition
   An Old Wedding Tradition

3. Read the article again. Are the sentences true (*T*) or false (*F*)?

   1. A bride in India has paint on her hands. ___
   2. A bride in India has blue paint in her hair. ___
   3. It is cold in the Omo Valley. ___
   4. Sports players never have colored hair. ___

4. **YOUR TURN** Work with a partner. Ask and answer the question.
   What are some sports and wedding traditions from your culture?

DID YOU KNOW…?
Face painting and body painting are thousands of years old. There are natural colors in things from the earth, like plants and clay. People use these for paint.

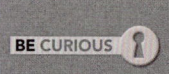

BE CURIOUS Find out about a traditional Indian wedding. What are some of the traditions? (Workbook, p. 73)

Discovery EDUCATION
1.3 A VERY INDIAN WEDDING

UNIT 1 REVIEW

Vocabulary

1. Label the photos with the correct categories.

art	food	places
clothing	music	sports

1. _____
2. _____ 
3. _____ 
4. _____ 
5. _____ 
6. _____ 

2. Complete the sentences with the correct words.

computer	hat	photo	TV
jacket	phone	shoes	watch

1. I have a _____ on my head.
2. I use my _____ to do my homework.
3. There are a lot of good shows on _____.
4. Lori is on the _____. Do you want to talk to her?
5. It's cold! I have on a _____ over my shirt.
6. See this _____ of my mother? It's from 1980!
7. Sam and Ann left their _____ by the door.
8. I don't have a _____, so I check the time on my phone.

Grammar

3. Circle the correct words.

Vicky: Hey, Paolo! ¹**Is / Are / Do / Does** you have an art class this year?

Paolo: Yes, I ²**am / am not / do / don't**. I ³**am / is / has / have** two art classes.

Vicky: ⁴**Is / Are / Do / Does** Mrs. Meyers one of your teachers?

Paolo: No, she ⁵**is / isn't / does / doesn't**. Why?

Vicky: Oh, she ⁶**is / isn't / does / doesn't** my aunt. She ⁷**is / are / has / have** three art classes this year.

Paolo: I see. My art teachers ⁸**is / are / has / have** Mr. Klein and Ms. Rodriguez.

4. Match the sentences with the same meaning.

1. It's my volleyball. ___
2. It's Sandra's dress. ___
3. It's Ted's pen. ___
4. It's your sandwich. ___

a. It's mine.
b. It's yours.
c. It's his.
d. It's hers.

Useful language

5. Circle the correct answers.

1. **A:** We have an unusual tradition in my family.
   B: Tell me _____ it.
   a. on   b. in   c. about

2. **A:** We always have a big dinner for my birthday.
   B: _____? Me, too.
   a. When   b. Really   c. Then

3. **A:** Why is your face green?
   B: Oh, it's for the soccer game.
   A: That's _____. Is green your school color?
   a. always   b. never   c. interesting

4. **A:** We always have a picnic at the park on Saturdays.
   B: Then _____?
   a. what   b. why   c. where
   A: We usually play games.

PROGRESS CHECK: Now I can . . .

☐ identify and talk about modern and traditional things.
☐ talk about modern and traditional things in my life.
☐ ask and answer questions about possessions.
☐ keep a conversation going.
☐ write about a family tradition.
☐ talk about sports, weddings, and other traditions.

2 WHAT'S Playing?

Discovery EDUCATION

BE CURIOUS

A Life on Broadway

What types of TV shows do you like watching?

Mumbai: From Computers to Film

Who's Real?

1. What are the people watching?

2. How do you think they feel about it?

3. Do you like to do this activity?

UNIT CONTENTS
Vocabulary Types of movies; types of TV shows
Grammar Simple present review; adverbs of frequency; verb + infinitive or *-ing* form (gerund)
Listening Deciding what to watch

Vocabulary: Types of movies

1. Match the phrases (a–i) with the correct movie posters.

a. an action movie
b. an animated movie
c. a comedy
✓ d. a drama
e. a fantasy movie
f. a horror movie
g. a martial arts movie
h. a musical
i. a romance movie

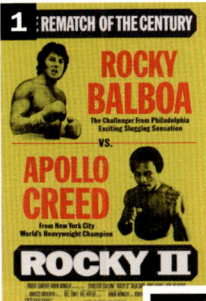

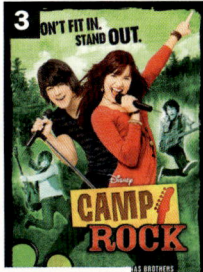

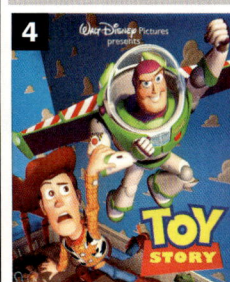

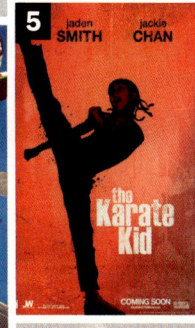

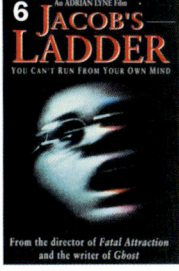

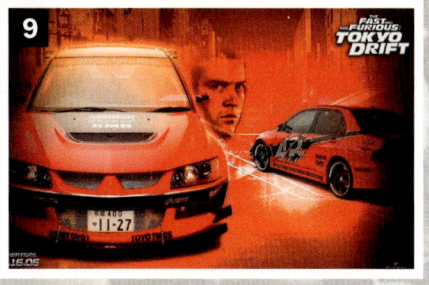

1. d
2. ___
3. ___
4. ___
5. ___
6. ___
7. ___
8. ___
9. ___

2. Listen, check, and repeat.

3. Write the types of movies.

1. A lot of things happen quickly in this type of movie. — *action movie*
2. The music in this type of film is great, and the actors are very good singers. — _____
3. People say these movies are for children, but adults watch them, too. — _____
4. This type of movie usually has events that couldn't happen in real life and great special effects. — _____
5. The story and characters in these movies are very funny. They make you laugh! — _____

Speaking: More movies

4. YOUR TURN Work with a partner. Name a movie for each type of movie.

> *Bend It Like Beckham* is a drama.

> *Twilight* is a drama, too. And it's also a romance movie.

5. What are some of your favorite movies? What types of movies are they?

> One of my favorite movies is *The Hunger Games*. It's a fantasy and an action movie. I also like . . .

Say it RIGHT!

The letters *sh*, *ci*, and *ti* can make the /ʃ/ sound. Listen to the sentence.

She liked the spe**ci**al effects in the ac**ti**on movie.

Listen to the words in Exercise 1 again. Which other word makes the /ʃ/ sound? What letters make the sound?

▶ Workbook, p. 8

Reading Cinema's Best Villains; My All-Time Favorite Movie; Hooray for Bollywood!
Conversation Asking for and giving opinions
Writing A movie review

Let's Go to the Movies!

Welcome to my blog about movies.

I sometimes go to the movies three times a week! How often do you go to the movies?

My favorite types of films are horror, action, and fantasy movies. What types of movies do you like?

I also love the "bad guys" in movies. Here are my top three villains.

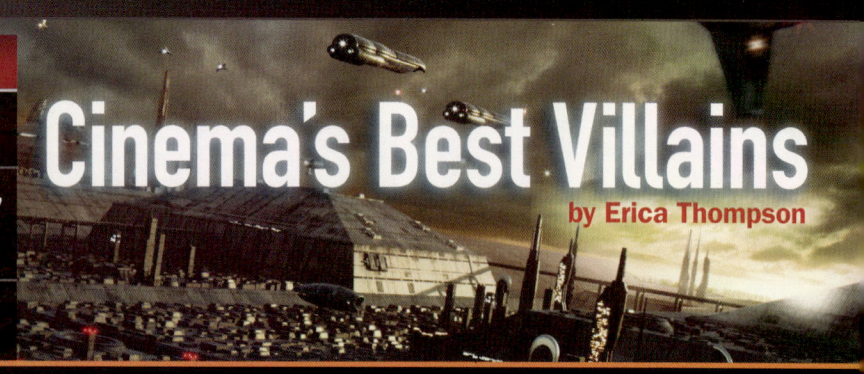

Cinema's Best Villains
by Erica Thompson

Cruella De Vil
Movie: *101 Dalmatians* **Actor:** Betty Lou Gerson (voice) **Famous phrase:** "You beasts!" I don't like this movie very much, but Cruella is a great villain. She loves puppies and especially Dalmatians – because she wants to wear them!

Darth Vader
Movie: *Star Wars V: The Empire Strikes Back* **Actor:** David Prowse **Famous phrase:** "You don't know the power of the dark side!" This is my favorite movie, and Darth Vader is the perfect villain because he never shows his face. He also speaks with a strange voice.

The Penguin
Movie: *Batman Returns* **Actor:** Danny DeVito **Famous phrase:** "Nyuk, nyuk, nyuk." The Penguin is a villain in some of the Batman movies, TV shows, and comic books. His real name is Oswold Cobblepot. Sometimes he's funny, and sometimes he's scary, but he's always dangerous. I like him best in *Batman Returns*.

Who is your favorite movie villain?

Reading: A blog about movie villains

1. Look at the photos of the three movie characters. What types of movies do you think they are from?

2. Read and listen to the blog post. Which of the movies that Erica writes about does she like?

3. Read the blog post again. Answer the questions.
   1. What types of movies does Erica like?
   _____
   2. Why does Cruella De Vil like puppies?
   _____
   3. Why does Erica think Darth Vader is a perfect villain?
   _____
   4. What is the Penguin's real name?
   _____
   5. Which movie doesn't Erica like? Which one is her favorite?
   _____

4. **YOUR TURN** Work with a partner. Do you agree with Erica's best villains? Who are your top three favorite movie villains? Why?

> One of my favorite villains is . . . because . . .

DID YOU KNOW...?
David Prowse was Darth Vader, but he didn't talk in the movie. Another actor, James Earl Jones, was Darth Vader's voice.

Grammar: Simple present review

5. Complete the chart.

Use the simple present to talk about routines, habits, and facts.

Wh- questions	Affirmative answers	Negative answers
What movies _____ you _____?	I **like** horror movies.	I **don't like** musicals.
How often **does** Erica **go** to the movies?	She _____ to the movies three times a week.	She _____ to the movies on Sundays.
Yes/No questions	**Short answers**	
Do you **like** horror movies?	Yes, I _____.	No, I **don't**.
_____ Erica _____ to the movies?	Yes, she **does**.	No, she _____.
Contractions do not = _____	does not = _____	

> Check your answers: Grammar reference, p. 107

6. Circle the correct words. Then answer the questions with information about you.

1. **Do** / Does you **go** / goes to the movies on the weekends?
   What types of movies **do** / does you **see** / sees?
   Yes, I do. I see action movies and comedies.

2. **What** / Where types of movies **do** / does your friends **like** / likes?
   Do / Does you **like** / likes the same types of movies?
   _____

3. **How** / When late **do** / does the movie theaters **stay** / stays open in your city?
   _____

> *Spell it* **RIGHT!**
>
> | I/you/we/they | he/she/it |
> |---|---|
> | go | go**es** |
> | study | stud**ies** |
> | teach | teach**es** |

7. Rewrite the sentences. Put the adverbs of frequency in the correct places.

1. Jamie watches movies with his friends. (usually)
   Jamie usually watches movies with his friends.

2. Amy buys popcorn at the movies. (always)
   _____

3. Carol reads movie reviews online. (sometimes)
   _____

4. I'm at the movie theater early. (often)
   _____

Adverbs of frequency

always   usually   often   sometimes   never

Adverbs of frequency usually come after the verb *be*, but before other verbs.
   I'm **never** late. They **never** learn.
Usually and *sometimes* may come before the subject.
   Sam **usually** goes to the movies three times a week.
   Usually, Sam goes to the movies three times a week.

Speaking: Movie-watching habits

8. YOUR TURN Work with a partner. Ask and answer questions about where and how often you watch movies.

> Where do you watch movies?

> I usually watch movies at the movie theater.

> I never watch movies at home.

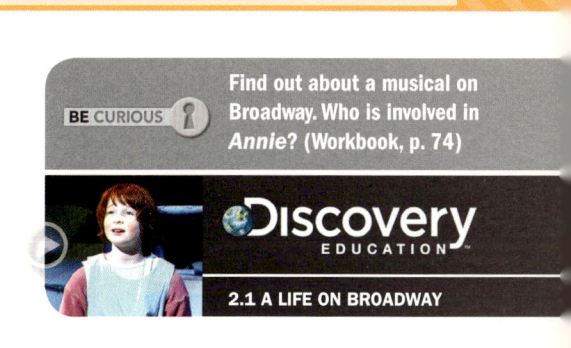

BE CURIOUS — Find out about a musical on Broadway. Who is involved in *Annie*? (Workbook, p. 74)

Discovery EDUCATION
2.1 A LIFE ON BROADWAY

> Workbook, p. 9

Unit 2 | 15

WHAT'S ON?

Listening: Deciding what to watch

1. Who do you watch TV with? What shows do you watch together?

2. Listen to Joanna and Alex decide what to watch on TV. What shows do they want to watch? Write *J* (Joanna), *A* (Alex), or *B* (both).

   1. *Big Brother* ___   2. *Elementary* ___   3. *The Big Bang Theory* ___

3. Listen again. Are the statements true (*T*) or false (*F*)?

   1. Sheldon and Leonard are scientists on a TV show. ___
   2. Penny is Joanna's neighbor. ___
   3. Alex saw *Big Brother* in the past. ___
   4. Joanna likes animated shows. ___
   5. Alex and Joanna both like dramas. ___

Vocabulary: Types of TV shows

4. Label the pictures with the correct words. Then listen and check your answers.

a cartoon	a game show	a soap opera
a crime series	a reality TV show	a talk show
✓ a documentary	a sitcom	the news

   1. *a documentary* 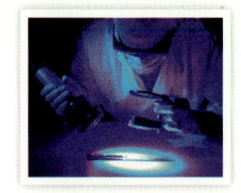   2.  _____   3. _____
   4.  _____   5.  _____   6. _____ 
   7.  _____   8.  _____   9. _____ 

5. **YOUR TURN** Work with a partner. Talk about how often you watch each type of TV show.

   > I never watch documentaries. I often watch crime series.

DID YOU KNOW...?
Sitcom is short for *situation comedy*.

Grammar: Verb + infinitive or -ing form (gerund)

6. Complete the chart.

Verb + infinitive	Verb + -ing form (gerund)
They **want to watch** a drama.	Sheldon **dislikes try**_____ new things.
He **needs** _____ **see** who gets voted off *Big Brother*.	Leonard **enjoys trying** different things.

Verb + infinitive or -ing form (gerund)
I **like to read** comic books. I **like reading** comic books.
They **love to read** comic books. They **love** _____ comic books.
She **hates to watch** reality TV shows. She **hates watching** reality TV shows.
He **prefers** _____ the news online. He **prefers getting** the news online.

> Check your answers: Grammar reference, p. 107

7. Complete the questions and answers with the *-ing* form (gerund) or infinitive of the verbs. Sometimes more than one answer is possible.

1. **A:** Do you want ___to get___ (get) this big screen TV?
   B: No. I hate _____ (pay) full price. Let's see if one is on sale.
2. **A:** I like _____ (watch) movies online.
   B: Not me. I prefer _____ (go) to a movie theater.
3. **A:** Ugh! I need _____ (wash) the dishes before we watch TV.
   B: Do you dislike _____ (do) them? I can help you.
4. **A:** Does your sister like _____ (work) for a TV studio?
   B: Yes. She loves _____ (think) of new ideas for TV shows.

8. YOUR TURN Use the words and your own ideas to write sentences that are true for you.

1. my parents / like / watch / . . . ___My parents like watching talk shows.___
2. my friends / enjoy / read / . . . _____
3. I / need / get / . . . _____
4. I / want / see / . . . _____

Get it RIGHT!

Use the infinitive or *-ing* form (gerund) of a verb, not the base form, after some verbs.
I **want to write** a TV show. NOT: ~~I want write~~ a TV show.
She **loves to watch** TV at night.
OR She **loves watching** TV at night.
NOT ~~She loves watch TV at night.~~

Speaking: TV-watching habits

9. YOUR TURN Read the sentences and check (✓) "Yes" or "No" in the "You" column.

	You		Your partner	
	Yes	No	Yes	No
I love watching sitcoms.				
I hate to watch documentaries.				
I want to watch less TV.				
I enjoy watching TV shows online.				

10. Work with a partner. Ask and answer questions about the information in Exercise 9. Check (✓) "Yes" or "No" in the "Your partner" column.

> Do you like watching sitcoms?

> No, I don't. I hate to watch sitcoms.

> Workbook, pp. 10–11

REAL TALK 2.2 WHAT TYPES OF TV SHOWS DO YOU LIKE WATCHING?

TV and Movie FAVORITES

Conversation: It's really funny!

1. **REAL TALK** Watch or listen to the teenagers. Check the shows they mention.

☐ animated movies	☐ documentaries	☐ horror movies	☐ soap operas
☐ cartoons	☐ dramas	☐ musicals	☐ sports news
☐ comedies	☐ game shows	☐ reality TV shows	☐ talk shows

2. **YOUR TURN** What types of TV shows do *you* like watching? Tell your partner.

3. Listen to Jay and Tina talking about TV shows. Complete the conversation.

   USEFUL LANGUAGE: Asking for and giving opinions
   How do you feel about   What do you think about   I think   In my opinion

   Jay: Do you watch a lot of TV, Tina?
   Tina: Yes, I do.
   Jay: What do you like to watch?
   Tina: I really like **sitcoms**.
   Jay: ¹_____ *Modern Family*?
   Tina: That's my favorite show! It's really **funny**!
   Jay: I like it, too. ²_____ **reality TV shows**?
   Tina: ³_____ they're **boring**. I never watch them. What about you?
   Jay: They're OK. I sometimes watch them, but I prefer **game shows**.
   Tina: Really? Why?
   Jay: ⁴_____, they're **exciting**.
   Tina: Yeah, I guess so.

4. Practice the conversation with a partner.

5. **YOUR TURN** Work with a partner. Practice the conversation in Exercise 3 again, but change the words in **purple**. Use the information in the chart for one conversation and your own ideas for another.

		My ideas
Type of 1st TV show	crime series	
Name of 1st TV show	CSI	
Description of 1st TV show	cool	
Type of 2nd TV show	soap operas	
Description of 2nd TV show	terrible	
Type of 3rd TV show	documentaries	
Description of 3rd TV show	interesting	

18 | Unit 2

My All-Time Favorite Movie
by Sofia Ramos

My favorite movie is *Twilight*, the first film in the Twilight Saga series. It stars Kristen Stewart as Bella and Robert Pattinson as Edward. The director is Catherine Hardwicke.

The movie is about Bella, a teenage girl in modern times. She moves to Forks, a small town in Washington. She meets Edward, a smart and good-looking classmate. She discovers he is a vampire, but she falls in love with him anyway. Another vampire wants to hurt Bella, so Edward tries to protect her.

I like this movie because the acting is really good. The music and camerawork make it dark and mysterious. I love watching fantasy movies, and this movie combines fantasy and romance.

Reading to write: A movie review

6. Look at the photo in Sofia's movie review. What type of movie do you think it is? Read the review to check.

Focus on CONTENT
When you write a movie review, include this information:
- the main characters and actors
- the time and place
- the director
- the type of movie
- a short description of the story
- why you like it or don't like it

7. Read Sofia's review again. What information from the Focus on Content box does she include in each paragraph?

Focus on LANGUAGE
Connectors *so* and *because*

Use **so** when one event is the result of another event:
- *Edward is smart and good-looking, **so** Bella falls in love with him.*

Use **because** to explain the reason something happens.
- *I like action movies **because** they are exciting.*

8. Find an example of *so* and an example of *because* in Sofia's review.

9. Complete the sentences with *so* or *because*.

1. Harry Potter has special powers, _____ he goes to the Hogwarts School for wizards.
2. Peter Parker becomes Spider-Man _____ a spider bites him.
3. In *Toy Story*, Woody and Buzz get lost, _____ they try to find their way home.
4. At the beginning of *The Lion King*, Simba is sad _____ his father dies.

Writing: Your movie review

PLAN
Choose your favorite movie or a movie you saw recently. Include the information in the Focus on Content box and take notes in a chart like the one below.

The main characters and actors	
The director	
The type of movie	
The time and place	
A short description of the story	
Why you like it or don't like it	

WRITE
Now, write your movie review. Use your notes to help you. Write at least 60 words.

CHECK
Check your writing. Can you answer "yes" to these questions?

- Is information from the Focus on Content box in your review?
- Do you use *so* and *because* to show how events connect?

Workbook, pp. 12–13

HOORAY for BOLLYWOOD!

Forget Hollywood! Bollywood is number one in the world of cinema! Bollywood is the name of the Hindi film industry in India. Its home is in Mumbai. Mumbai's name was Bombay in the past, so Bollywood gets its name from *Bombay* and *Hollywood*. Bollywood makes about 1,000 movies every year. That's about two times more than Hollywood. More people watch Bollywood movies, too – over three billion people watch them! About 14 million Indians go to the movies every day.

Bollywood movies are different from Hollywood movies. They are very long and usually last about three or four hours. Many of them are musicals. The movie *Indra Sabha* has the record for the most songs. It has 71 songs in it.

Music and dancing are very important in Bollywood movies. They often contain typical Indian music and traditional Indian dance styles, like Kathak and Bharata Natyam. The dancing helps tell the story in the movie. Bollywood movies also contain modern dance forms, like hip-hop and jazz. The films often include romance, comedy, action, and adventure in their stories.

These movies aren't only popular in India. People around the world love watching them! The movies are usually in Hindi, but there are often subtitles in other languages, like Bengali, Arabic, and English.

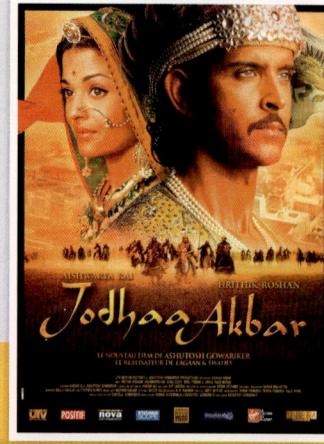

Culture: Bollywood movies

1. Look at the photos. What types of movies do think they are?

2. Read and listen to the article. Check the best description of Bollywood movies.

   ☐ Traditional Indian movies in several languages
   ☐ Hindi movies, often with singing and dancing
   ☐ Hollywood movies made into Indian movies

3. Read the article again. Are the sentences *T* (true) or *F* (false)? Correct the false sentences.

   1. Bollywood is a combination of the words *Bengali* and *Hollywood*. ___
   2. More people go to see Bollywood movies than Hollywood movies. ___
   3. A lot of Bollywood movies are musicals. ___
   4. *Indra Sabha* has the record for the longest movie. ___
   5. Kathak is a type of traditional Indian music. ___
   6. Bollywood movies are popular in many countries. ___

4. **YOUR TURN** Work with a partner. Ask and answer the questions.

   1. Do you want to see a Bollywood movie? Why or why not?
   2. Do you watch Hollywood movies? How often?
   3. Do you prefer to watch Hollywood movies or movies from other countries? What is better about the movies you prefer?

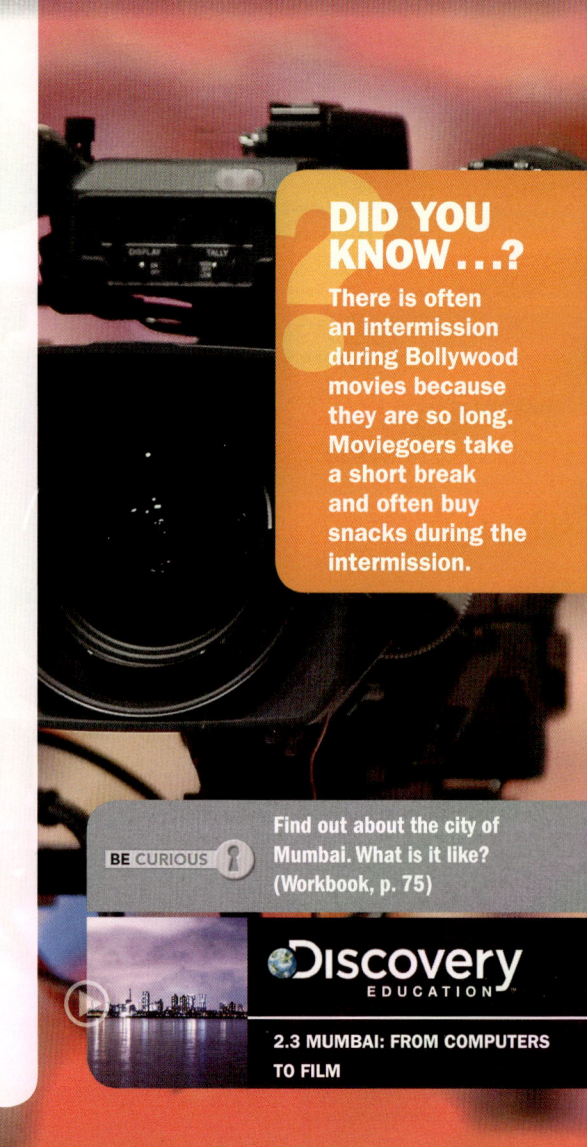

DID YOU KNOW...?

There is often an intermission during Bollywood movies because they are so long. Moviegoers take a short break and often buy snacks during the intermission.

BE CURIOUS Find out about the city of Mumbai. What is it like? (Workbook, p. 75)

Discovery EDUCATION
2.3 MUMBAI: FROM COMPUTERS TO FILM

UNIT 2 REVIEW

Vocabulary

1. **Put the letters in the correct order to make words for different types of movies.**

   1. aonercm _____
   2. meydoc _____
   3. nafstya _____
   4. roorhr _____

2. **Match the types of TV shows to their descriptions.**

   1. a talk show ___
   2. a game show ___
   3. the news ___
   4. a soap opera ___
   5. a crime series ___

a	Police officer Jules Kiln finds new clues to an old mystery on *The Scene*.
b	Today on *Green Street*, Sam is unhappy with Gina. Tara tells Mick her secret.
c	Tom Buckley speaks to the children of famous musicians on *Tell Me Today*.
d	Sarah Carver gives today's top events and weather at 8:00 p.m.
e	Watch three people try to win $25,000 on *Make It Big*.

Grammar

3. **Complete the sentences with the simple present forms of the verbs.**

do	not like	watch	go

   1. We usually _____ TV in the evening. Our favorite shows are sitcoms.
   2. Casey always _____ to the movies on the weekends.
   3. When _____ you usually _____ your homework?
   4. Vicky _____ soap operas. She thinks they're boring.

4. **Circle the correct answers. Sometimes both answers are correct.**

   1. Greg loves **to watch** / **watching** sitcoms at night.
   2. Sandra and Kelly want **to see** / **seeing** that new animated movie.
   3. I need **to leave** / **leaving** the theater right after the movie.
   4. Liv dislikes **to have** / **having** the TV on when she does her homework.

Useful language

5. **Circle the correct answers.**

   Jan: Hey, Doug. How do you [1]**think** / **feel** / **tell** about reality TV shows?

   Doug: In my [2]**thought** / **opinion** / **decision**, they're terrible.

   Jan: Really? I like them.

   Doug: Not me. I [3]**agree** / **dislike** / **think** they're boring.

   Jan: Well, I'm going to be on a reality TV show! How do you [4]**think** / **feel** / **tell** about that?

   Doug: Oh, uh, well . . . that's cool, I guess.

PROGRESS CHECK: Now I can . . .
- ☐ identify different types of movies.
- ☐ talk about my movie-watching habits.
- ☐ talk about different types of TV shows, preferences, and TV habits.
- ☐ ask for and give opinions.
- ☐ write a movie review.
- ☐ compare Hollywood movies with other movies.

▶ REVIEW UNITS 1–2, Workbook, pp. 14–15

CLIL PROJECT

2.4 Who's Real?, p. 116

3 Spending Habits

Discovery EDUCATION
BE CURIOUS

- Unusual Fun
- How do you spend your money?
- Zero: Past and Present

1. What do you think the people have in their bags?

2. Do you like to shop alone or with friends? Why?

3. How often do you go shopping? What do you usually buy?

UNIT CONTENTS

Vocabulary Places to shop; money verbs
Grammar Present continuous review; simple present vs. present continuous; quantifiers
Listening Shopping habits

Vocabulary: Places to shop

1. Complete the key in the map with the correct numbers.

_7_ bank and ATM
___ bookstore
___ clothing store
___ department store
___ electronics store
___ food court
___ jewelry store
___ music store
___ pharmacy
___ shoe store
___ sporting goods store

2. Listen, check, and repeat.

3. What things are there in each place in Exercise 1?

> There are jeans, T-shirts, and jackets in a clothing store.

> A clothing store also has hats, dresses, and . . .

NOTICE IT
ATM stands for *automated teller machine*. A *teller* is a person in a bank whose job is to receive money from or give money to customers.

Speaking: Your favorite stores

4. YOUR TURN Work with a partner. What are your three favorite stores? Why?

> One of my favorite stores is a department store. There are many different things for sale there. Another favorite store is . . .

5. Now work with the class. Make a list of everyone's favorite stores. Which stores are the top three favorites?

▶ Workbook, p. 16

Say it RIGHT!
In one-word compound nouns, the first syllable is stressed. In compound nouns with two or more words, the first syllable of the first word is usually stressed. Listen and repeat the words.

bookstore   **jew**elry store   **spor**ting goods store

Listen and circle the stressed syllable in each compound noun.
food court   music store
clothing store   shoe store

Reading A Day at the Mall in Dubai; Product Reviews; Adopt an Animal
Conversation Making requests when shopping
Writing A product review

Unit 3 | 23

STORES and MORE

A Day at the Mall in DUBAI

I'm Lucas. I'm from Mexico, but I live in Dubai now because my parents work here. I'm writing about my life in my new city.

Today, I'm at the Dubai Mall with my family. It has about 1,200 stores, including five department stores, two music stores, more than 25 electronics stores, and about 50 shoe stores!

Are we shopping? No, we're not! There are a lot of other things to do at this mall. My dad and my sister are watching the fish in the Aquarium and Underwater Zoo right now. There are more than 33,000 fish – even sharks! My mom and I are skating on the Olympic-size Dubai Ice Rink. It's hot in Dubai, but it's cold at the ice rink! Later, I want to go to the mall's theme park, the Sega Republic. It has 170 games and many rides.

Outside of the mall is the Dancing Fountain. The water goes up 150 meters! At night, the water changes color because the fountain has lights with 25 different colors.

I hope we stay here all day and night!

Reading: An article about a mall in Dubai

1. Look at the photos. What do you see?

2. Read and listen to the article. Match the photos (a–d) with the places (1–4).

   1. The Aquarium and Underwater Zoo ___
   2. The Dubai Ice Rink ___
   3. Stores in the mall ___
   4. The Dancing Fountain ___

3. Read the article again. Complete the sentences with the correct numbers.

   1. The mall has about _____ stores.
   2. There are about _____ shoe stores in the mall.
   3. The aquarium has over _____ fish.
   4. There are _____ games at the theme park.
   5. The water in the fountain goes up _____ meters.
   6. There are _____ different colors in the fountain lights.

4. **YOUR TURN** Work with a partner. What would you do at the Dubai Mall? Why?

   I'd go to the ice rink. I like to ice-skate!

DID YOU KNOW...?
The Dubai Mall is one of the biggest malls in the world. More than 50 million people visit it every year.

Grammar: Present continuous review; simple present vs. present continuous

5. Complete the chart.

Use the present continuous to talk about activities that are happening now.

Wh- questions	Affirmative answers	Negative answers
What **are** you **doing**?	I _____ **writing** a book.	**I'm not writing** about my job.
What **is** he _____?	**He's skating**.	**He's** _____ **running**.
What _____ they **doing**?	**They're watch**___ TV.	**They** _____ **skating**.
Yes/No questions	**Short answers**	
_____ you **writing** about Dubai?	Yes, I _____.	No, **I'm** _____.
_____ he **skating**?	Yes, he _____.	No, he **isn't**.
Are we **shopping**?	Yes, we **are**.	No, we _____.

Remember: Use the simple present for facts, habits, and routines.
At night, the water **changes** color. = routine
Look! The water **is changing** color. = activity happening now

> Check your answers: Grammar reference, p. 108

6. Complete the sentences with the present continuous forms of the verbs.

1. Cassandra _____ (write) a blog about her life in the city.
2. What _____ you _____ (buy) at the electronics store?
3. I _____ (wait) in line at the pharmacy.
4. We _____ (not shop) at the mall today.
5. Marta _____ (not get) money at the ATM now.

> **Spell it RIGHT!**
> The **-ing** form:
> For verbs ending in **-e**, remove the **e**, and then add **-ing**: *write* → *writing*.
> For verbs ending with one vowel and one consonant, double the final consonant: *shop* → *shopping*.

7. Complete the conversation with the simple present or the present continuous forms of the verbs.

Abe: Hi, Lori. What ¹ *are* you *doing* (do)?
Lori: I ² _____ (shop) with my parents. We ³ _____ (look) for a new school bag and clothes at a department store.
Abe: Just in time! School starts on Monday.
Lori: I know. We ⁴ _____ (do) the same thing every year. We always ⁵ _____ (shop) the weekend before school starts.
Abe: I ⁶ _____ (not do) that! I ⁷ _____ (buy) my things for school online during the summer.
Lori: That's a good idea! So, what ⁸ _____ you _____ (do) right now?
Abe: I ⁹ _____ (watch) a movie on TV.
Lori: Lucky you!

Speaking: At the mall

8. YOUR TURN Work with a partner. You are at a mall in different stores. Think of at least five questions you can ask each other on the phone. Use the simple present and present continuous.

> Where are you? What are you doing? Why . . . ?

9. Create a conversation with your partner.

> Where are you? What are you doing?

> I'm in the shoe store. I'm looking for new sneakers. I want …

BE CURIOUS — Find out about places in Dubai. What are some things people do in Dubai? (Workbook, p. 76)

Discovery EDUCATION
3.1 UNUSUAL FUN

Workbook, p. 17

Unit 3 | 25

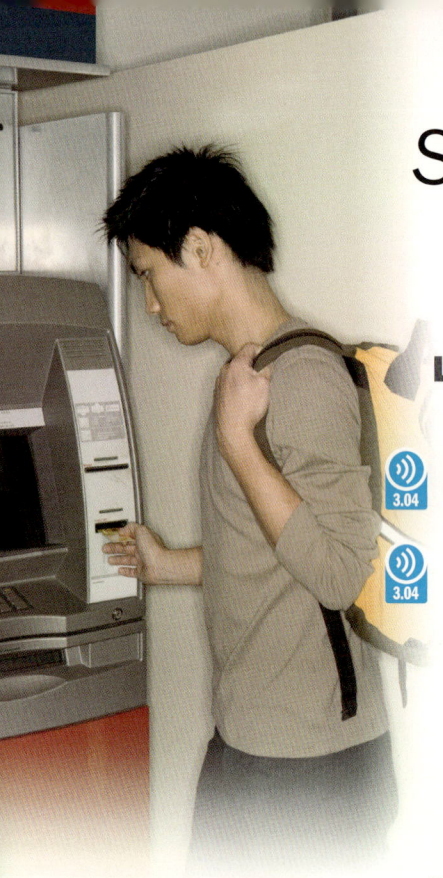

Spending and SAVING

Listening: Shopping habits

1. Do you usually shop at stores or online? Why?

2. Listen to a reporter talk to teens about shopping and money. What do Josh and Megan have in their shopping bags?

3. Listen again. Circle the correct answers.
   1. Josh wants **a new video game** / **a T-shirt**.
   2. Josh usually buys clothes **at a mall** / **online**.
   3. It's **Megan's** / **Josh's** birthday.
   4. Megan has a **necklace** / **soccer ball** for herself.
   5. Megan wants a new **job** / **phone**.

Vocabulary: Money verbs

4. Look at the pictures. Complete the sentences with the simple present forms of the verbs. Then listen and check your answers.

✓ borrow	earn	save	withdraw
deposit	lend	spend	

   Jordan's friend is selling a bike. It costs $200. Jordan wants to buy the bike, but he only has $50. He ¹_____borrows_____ money from his aunt. His aunt ²_____ him $50. He ³_____ the money in his bank account. He gets a part-time job at a pizza place in the food court, and he ⁴_____ $100 a week. He ⁵_____ some of that money on movies and video games. He ⁶_____ $25 a week for a month and puts it in the bank. Finally, he ⁷_____ $200 from the bank, and he buys his friend's bike!

5. **YOUR TURN** Work with a partner. Ask and answer the questions.
   1. Do you earn money? How do you earn it?
   2. Do you usually save money or spend money? What do you spend money on?
   3. Do you ever borrow money? Who lends you money?
   4. Do you ever lend money? Who borrows money from you?
   5. Where do you or your parents deposit and withdraw money?

Grammar: Quantifiers

6. Complete the chart.

Use quantifiers to show the amount of something.	
With countable plural nouns	**With uncountable nouns**
How **many** T-shirts do you have?	How **much** money do you have?
I have **some** / _____ / **enough** T-shirts.	I have _____ / **a lot of** / **enough** money.
I don't have **many** / _____ / **a lot of** / **enough** T-shirts.	I don't have **much** / **any** / **a lot of** / _____ money.
Are there **many** / **any** / _____ / **enough** T-shirts in your dresser?	Is there _____ / **any** / **a lot of** / **enough** money in your bank account?
Yes, there are. / No, there aren't.	Yes, there is. / No, there isn't.

> **Get it RIGHT!**
>
> **enough** = as many as needed
> **not enough** = less than what is needed
> **Enough** goes before nouns and after adjectives:
> I don't have **enough money** to buy a phone.
> I'm not **old enough** to get a job.

> Check your answers: Grammar reference, p. 108

7. Circle the correct words.

1. Cynthia has **much** / **(a lot of)** money.
2. I save **some** / **any** money every month.
3. Are there **much** / **any** department stores in that mall?
4. How **much** / **many** time do you spend at the mall?
5. I'm not old **some** / **enough** to drive a car.
6. There aren't **a lot of** / **much** cars for sale here.

8. Complete the conversation with the correct words.

a lot of	enough	how much	✓ any	some

Eddie: Oh, no! The bus is coming, and I don't have ¹ _**any**_ money. Can I borrow ² _____ money from you?

Maya: Well, I don't have ³ _____ money. I only have $5. ⁴ _____ is a ticket?

Eddie: It's $2.50.

Maya: Oh, OK. I have ⁵ _____ money, so I can lend you $2.50. No problem.

Eddie: Thanks!

Speaking: A money quiz

9. **YOUR TURN** Read the questions and use the words to write answers that are true for you. Then add one more question to the list. Write the answers.

a lot of   some   enough   not enough   not any

1. How much money do you save a month? _____
2. How many times do you go shopping each month? _____
3. How much do you spend on clothes each month? _____
4. _____

10. Work with a partner. Ask and answer the questions from Exercise 9.

> How much money do you save a month?
>
> I don't save any money. How much money do you save?
>
> I save a lot of money.

Workbook, pp. 18–19

REAL TALK 3.2 HOW DO YOU SPEND YOUR MONEY?

What We BUY

Conversation: Shopping time

1. **REAL TALK** Watch or listen to the teenagers. Check the things they spend money on.

   - ☐ a video game
   - ☐ birthday gifts for friends
   - ☐ bus tickets
   - ☐ clothes
   - ☐ comic books
   - ☐ food
   - ☐ jewelry
   - ☐ music
   - ☐ plans with friends
   - ☐ shoes
   - ☐ sporting goods
   - ☐ things for a cell phone

2. **YOUR TURN** How do *you* spend *your* money? Tell your partner.

3. Listen to Lisa talking with a store clerk. Complete the conversation.

USEFUL LANGUAGE: Making requests when shopping

I'd like to buy   I'd prefer   I'll take it!   Can I try it on?

Lisa:	Excuse me. ¹_____ **a dress**.
Clerk:	OK. How about this **blue dress**? It's new.
Lisa:	²_____ a different color. Does it come in **black**?
Clerk:	Yes, it does. Here it is.
Lisa:	Nice. How much is it?
Clerk:	It's **$49**.
Lisa:	³_____
Clerk:	Of course. What size do you wear?
Lisa:	**Size 8**.
Clerk:	OK. What do you think?
Lisa:	Actually, it's not big enough. I need a larger size.
Clerk:	OK. Try **a 10**. How is it?
Lisa:	Great. ⁴_____

4. Practice the conversation with a partner.

5. **YOUR TURN** Repeat the conversation in Exercise 3, but change the words in purple. Use the information in the chart for one conversation and your own ideas for another.

		My ideas
Item	a sweater	
First color	red	
Second color	green	
Price	$35	
First size	a small	
Second size	a medium	

A WARM JACKET!

by Wayne, October 16
★★★★☆

The K-Light Jacket is a great jacket. The jacket is at Tom's Sporting Goods Store in a lot of colors. It costs $49.99. The jacket is warm, and it's good for hikes in cooler weather. It's not warm enough for very cold weather. Buy this jacket today. Wear it on your next hike! Note: Don't buy your usual size. I usually wear a medium, but I have this jacket in a large.

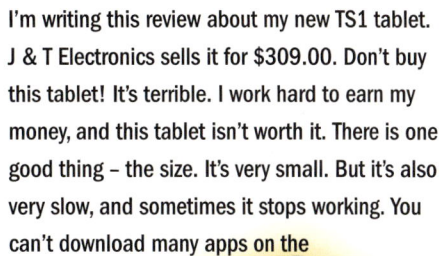

A TERRIBLE TABLET!

by Victoria, December 2
★☆☆☆☆

I'm writing this review about my new TS1 tablet. J & T Electronics sells it for $309.00. Don't buy this tablet! It's terrible. I work hard to earn my money, and this tablet isn't worth it. There is one good thing – the size. It's very small. But it's also very slow, and sometimes it stops working. You can't download many apps on the tablet. Save your money! Don't spend it on this awful product.

Reading to write: Product reviews

6. Look at the reviews. Do you think the people like the products? Read the reviews to check.

> *Focus on* **CONTENT**
> When you write a product review, include:
> - the name of the product
> - the price
> - what you like about it
> - what you don't like about it
> - where you can buy it
> - your recommendation

7. Read Wayne's and Victoria's reviews again. Find examples for the categories in the Focus on Content box for each review.

> *Focus on* **LANGUAGE**
> You can use the imperative to make recommendations. Use the base form of a verb for affirmative sentences. Use *don't* with the base form of a verb in negative sentences.
> - **Buy** this TV now! **Don't buy** that TV!
> - **Get** the new Lazer cell phone today. **Don't get** the new Starz cell phone.

8. Find examples of imperatives in Wayne's and Victoria's reviews.

9. Put the words in the correct order to make sentences with the imperative. Write an affirmative and a negative sentence for each item.

at home or work / use / this cell phone

1. _____
2. _____

on this book / money / spend

3. _____
4. _____

Writing: Your product review

▢ **PLAN**
Choose a product you have. Write notes about it.

Name	
Where to buy it	
Price	
What you like	
What you don't like	
Recommendation	

▢ **WRITE**
Write a review about the product. Use your notes to help you. Write at least 60 words.

▢ **CHECK**
Check your writing. Can you answer "yes" to these questions?

- Is information for each category from the Focus on Content box in your review?
- Do you use the imperative correctly?

Adopt an ANIMAL

Students around the world are saving their money, and then they're saving animals!

One way students save an animal is to "adopt" one. This means students give money to an organization. The organization uses the students' money to help animals. The students get a photo of the animal and information about it. For example, some students adopt tigers. They give money to an organization that helps tigers in Asia. Other students adopt whales. They look at photos of whales online, and they choose a whale to help. The whales have names! Students get a photo of the whale, and they can also see how the whale is doing online.

Mrs. Monson's students are adopting an animal in another way. They're helping a cat without a home. Now, the cat is living in their classroom! Her name is Shadow. She eats a lot of food, and she needs to see a vet. The students are having a bake sale and selling cakes and cookies. They're using the money to feed and take care of Shadow. Shadow plays when the students are working! She sleeps in the classroom, too. At the end of the year, one student gets to keep Shadow!

Culture: Students helping animals

1. Look at the photos. What animals do you see? Where do they live?

2. Read and listen to the article. What does it mean to adopt a pet?

3. Read the article again. Are the sentences *T* (true) or *F* (false)? Correct the false sentences.

   1. An organization helps tigers in the United States. ___
   2. An organization helps whales in the ocean. ___
   3. The tigers have names. ___
   4. Students get a photo of the animal they help. ___
   5. Shadow is living at a school. ___
   6. Shadow doesn't eat enough food. ___

4. **YOUR TURN** Work with a partner. Answer the questions.

   1. Do you know anyone who earns or saves money to help people or animals? What do they do?
   2. How could you earn money to help people or animals? What people or animals would you help?

DID YOU KNOW...?

Many students in the United States have bake sales to earn money. They make food and sell it at school events. They spend the money on different things, like adopting an animal or buying sports uniforms.

BE CURIOUS Find out about the number zero. Who created it? (Workbook, p. 77)

Discovery EDUCATION

3.3 ZERO: PAST AND PRESENT

UNIT 3 REVIEW

Vocabulary

1. **Where do you buy or get these things? Label the pictures with the correct places.**

a bank	a food court	a pharmacy
a bookstore	a music store	a sporting goods store

   1. _____
   2. _____ 
   3. _____ 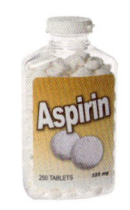
   4. _____ 
   5. _____ 
   6. _____ 

Grammar

2. **Complete the sentences with the present continuous or simple present forms.**

   1. Kyle _____ coffee at the café every morning.
   2. What _____ you usually _____ at a department store?
   3. Why _____ they always _____ money inside the bank instead of at an ATM?
   4. Peter _____ his birthday money right now.

3. **Circle the correct answers.**

   1. There aren't **much** / **many** shoe stores at the mall.
   2. Are there **much** / **many** watches at the jewelry store?
   3. I don't have **some** / **enough** time to go to the ATM.
   4. Do you want to eat **some** / **enough** food now?

Useful language

4. **Complete the conversation with the correct sentences and phrases.**

I'd like to buy	I'd prefer
I'll take them!	Can I try them on?

   Jack: Hello. ¹_____ some new pants.

   Clerk: OK. How about these blue pants?

   Jack: ²_____ brown pants.

   Clerk: OK. We have these in brown. What size do you need?

   Jack: A medium, I think.
   ³_____

   Clerk: Sure. Take a medium and a large. So, do you like them?

   Jack: Yes, the medium pants are good.
   ⁴_____

PROGRESS CHECK: Now I can . . .

- ☐ identify places to shop.
- ☐ talk about the things I do every day and the things I'm doing now.
- ☐ ask and answer questions about spending and saving money.
- ☐ make requests when shopping.
- ☐ write a product review.
- ☐ talk about using money to help people or animals.

4 Our HEROES

Discovery EDUCATION
BE CURIOUS

- Wildlife Hero
- Who is your role model and why?
- The Chilean Mine Rescue
- Amelia Earhart: Famous Flyer

1. What are the people doing?
2. How do you think the boy feels about the man?
3. Who are some people you feel this way about?

UNIT CONTENTS

Vocabulary Cool jobs; adjectives of personality
Grammar Simple past statements review and *ago*; simple past questions review and *ago*
Listening Interview with a teenage hero

Vocabulary: Cool jobs

1. Label the pictures with the correct jobs.

an actor	a painter	a singer	✓ a writer
a dancer	a runner	a soccer player	
a lawyer	a scientist	a tennis player	

NOTICE IT
The word *actor* can be used for both men and women. The word *actress* is sometimes used for women.

1. _a writer_  2. 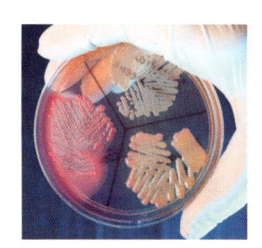 _____ 3.  _____ 4.  _____ 5. _____

6.  _____ 7.  _____ 8.  _____ 9.  _____ 10. _____

2. Listen, check, and repeat.

3. Write the jobs in the correct places in the chart.

Sports	Arts and Entertainment	Academic
	a writer	

Say it RIGHT!
The letter *i* can make the short *i* sound /ɪ/. It can also make the long *i* sound /aɪ/. Listen to the sentence. The first *i* in *scientist* is long. The second *i* is short.

/aɪ/ /ɪ/
My parents are scientists.

Listen to the jobs again. Which other words have a short *i* (/ɪ/)? Which ones have a long *i* (/aɪ/)?

Speaking: Who does that job?

4. **YOUR TURN** Work with a partner. Can you think of a person (a family member, a friend, or a famous person) for each job?

> My uncle is a lawyer.

> My mom is a lawyer, too.

5. Would you like these jobs? Why or why not?

> I'd like to be a writer. I want to write short stories.

> I wouldn't like to be a writer. I don't like to work alone.

▶ Workbook, p. 22

Reading Young and Talented!; My Hero; The Island of Champions
Conversation Asking for and giving clarification
Writing A description of a person you admire

Unit 4 | 33

SUPERSTARS

Home | Contact | About Us

Young and Talented!

From sports and music to technology and film, today's stars are young and talented! These young people are at the top of their professions. Find out why!

Javier "Chicharito" Hernández was born in Guadalajara, Mexico. He started playing soccer when he was seven. At 15, he signed his first professional contract. In 2010, he moved to England to play for Manchester United. He won an award for Most Valuable Player (MVP) in 2011 when he was 23 years old. He now plays for both Manchester United and the Mexican national team.

Nick D'Aloisio was born in Australia, but he grew up in London, England. He got his first computer when he was nine, and he wrote his first app at 12. In 2013, at 17, he sold an app to Yahoo for 30 million dollars! He also got a job with the company.

Beyoncé won her first talent show when she was seven and joined her first band, Girl's Tyme, when she was eight. This band later became Destiny's Child. In 2001, she became a solo singer. She made her first solo album in 2003. She is now one of the best-paid singers in the world, and she also acts.

? DID YOU KNOW...?

Talent often runs in the family. Javier Hernández's father and grandfather were professional soccer players. Beyoncé's sister is also a singer and actress.

Reading: A web page about young stars

1. Look at the photos. Do you know these people? What are their jobs?

2. Read and listen to the article. At what age did each person take the first step to his or her future job? What was the first step?

3. Read the article again. Complete the sentences with *Nick D'Aloisio*, *Javier Hernández*, or *Beyoncé*.

    1. _____ and _____ won awards for their talents.
    2. _____ became a millionaire at age 17.
    3. _____ worked with a group and then worked alone.
    4. _____ and _____ moved to different countries.
    5. _____ got a job with a famous company.

4. **YOUR TURN** Work with a partner. Think of a famous person from your country who is alive today. What does he or she do? What is he or she famous for?

> Diego Luna is a famous actor from Mexico City. He's famous for TV shows in Mexico and for movies in Mexico and in the United States.

Grammar: Simple past statements review and *ago*

5. Complete the chart.

Use simple past statements to describe things in the past and to talk about past events and activities. Use *ago* to say how far back in the past something happened or was.

	Affirmative statements	Negative statements
be	He _____ MVP in 2011. They **were** in Brazil a week **ago**.	He **wasn't** MVP in 2010. They **weren't** in Spain last week.
Regular verbs	He _____ for Mexico. I **moved** a month **ago**.	He **didn't play** for Spain. I _____ last week.
Irregular verbs	She _____ a solo album in 2003. I **got** a tablet a year _____.	She **didn't make** an album in 2001. I _____ a laptop.

> *Spell it* **RIGHT!**
>
> For regular verbs:
> + **-ed**: work → work**ed**
> + **-d**: live → liv**ed**
> **-y** → **-i** + **-ed**: try → tr**ied**
> double consonant + **-ed**: shop → shop**ped**
> For irregular verbs: See p. 121.

> Check your answers: Grammar reference, p. 109

6. Circle the correct words.

1. Gene Kelly (was) / were a famous dancer, actor, and singer.
2. I wasn't / weren't very good at singing when I was / were young.
3. You wasn't / weren't in class when the famous writer was / were there.
4. The Olympic runner was / were very tired after the race.

7. Rewrite the sentences in the simple past. Add the phrases in parentheses. The verbs in blue are irregular. Check the correct forms of those verbs on page 121.

1. John wants to be a professional tennis player. (10 years ago)

   John wanted to be a professional tennis player 10 years ago.

2. You **write** great short stories. (last year)

   _____

3. Lorena **is getting** a job as a lawyer. (last week)

   _____

4. I **sing** in a band. (in 2012)

   _____

5. The scientists don't work in the lab. (a week ago)

   _____

6. The runners are shopping for new shoes. (yesterday)

   _____

> *Get it* **RIGHT!**
>
> Remember that you do not add **-ed** to the end of irregular verbs in the simple past.
> She **sang** alone. NOT: ~~She singed alone.~~

Speaking: Who is it?

8. YOUR TURN Think of a famous person. Write five facts about his/her life. Use the suggestions or your own ideas.

| where he/she was born | when he/she became famous | an award he/she won |
| his/her job | how old he/she is | |

9. Work with a group. Tell your group about your famous person. Can they guess who it is?

> She was born in Mexico. She is a singer, and she started singing when she was nine years old. She also acted in soap operas. She . . .

Is it Thalía?   Yes, it is!

> **BE CURIOUS** Find out about a wildlife hero. What is her job? (Workbook, p. 78)
>
> **Discovery EDUCATION**
> 4.1 WILDLIFE HERO

> Workbook, p. 23

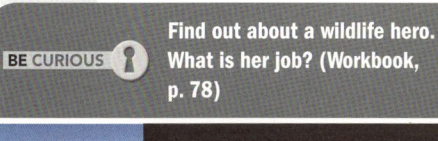

Being BRAVE

Listening: Interview with a teenage hero

1. Did you see or help in an emergency in the past? What happened?

2. Listen to Marcos talk to a news reporter. What was the emergency? What did Marcos do?

3. Listen again and circle the correct answers.
   1. Marcos was **in his house / outside** when the fire started.
   2. He saw **smoke / a strange light** in the sky.
   3. Max was **in the house / outside**.
   4. **Marcos / Max's dad** saw a ladder in the yard.
   5. Marcos **broke / opened** the window.
   6. Max climbed **down the ladder / into Marcos's arms**.

Vocabulary: Adjectives of personality

4. Match the pictures with the correct sentences. Then listen and check your answers.
   1. _a_ George is very **quiet**. He doesn't talk a lot.
   2. ___ Katy's really **funny**. She makes me laugh a lot.
   3. ___ Lou is very **serious**. He studies all the time.
   4. ___ Martina's really **brave**. She isn't scared of anything!
   5. ___ Leticia is so **cheerful**. She's so happy and always smiles.
   6. ___ Julia was **calm** during the emergency. She didn't get excited, and she called the police right away.
   7. ___ Brett is really **friendly**. He likes to meet new people.
   8. ___ Tonya is very **kind** to animals. She helped a cat get down from a tree.
   9. ___ Sometimes, Isabel is **stubborn**. She doesn't listen to her sister.

5. **YOUR TURN** Work with a partner. In what situations do the adjectives describe you?

   > I'm calm and brave in an emergency. I'm usually friendly at parties. I'm . . .

Grammar: Simple past questions review and *ago*

6. Complete the chart.

Use simple past questions to ask about past things, events, and activities.
Use ago to ask how far back in the past something happened or was.

	Wh- questions and answers	Yes/No questions and answers
be	How **was** he an hour _____? He **was** happy. Where **were** they? They _____ at home.	_____ he happy an hour **ago**? Yes, he **was**. / No, he **wasn't**. **Were** they at home? Yes, they _____. / No, they **weren't**.
Regular verbs	How long **ago did** it **start**? It **started** an hour **ago**. Why _____ you _____ him? I **carried** him because he was hurt.	**Did** it **start** an hour **ago**? Yes, it **did**. / No, it _____. _____ you **carry** him? Yes, I _____. / No, I **didn't**.
Irregular verbs	What _____ you _____? I **saw** a fire. Where **did** they **put** the ladder? They **put** it against the house.	**Did** you **see** a fire? Yes, I _____. / No, I **didn't**. **Did** they **put** the ladder against the house? Yes, they **did**. / No, they _____.

> Check your answers: Grammar reference, p. 109

7. Complete the sentences with the simple past forms of the verbs.

1. When _were_ you scared in the past? Why _____ you scared? (be)
2. _____ your friends ever _____ a fire? When _____ they _____ it? (see)
3. When _____ one of your friends brave? _____ you with him or her? (be)
4. _____ you _____ a stranger in the past? Who _____ you _____? (help)

8. Work with a partner. Ask and answer the questions in Exercise 7.

> When were you scared in the past? Why were you scared?

> I was scared last night. It was dark and stormy outside.

9. Complete the conversations with the simple past forms of the verbs.

✓ go   see   talk   think

1. **A:** _Did_ you _go_ out last night?
   B: Yes, I did. I saw my cousin play tennis. She's a great tennis player.
2. **A:** Who _____ you _____ to at the party?
   B: To Sam and Patricia. They were very friendly.
3. **A:** _____ you _____ Carl in class?
   B: No, but I saw him about an hour ago. He was really cheerful.

Speaking: I was brave!

10. YOUR TURN Work with a partner. Ask and answer questions about a time you were brave. Use one of the suggestions or your own idea.

| you helped someone in danger | you did something you were afraid to do | you gave a presentation |

When were you brave? What happened? What did you do?

> When were you brave?

> I was brave last month. I went outside in the dark to find our cat.

> Workbook, pp. 24–25

REAL TALK | 4.2 WHO IS YOUR ROLE MODEL AND WHY?

People WE ADMIRE

Conversation: Everyday heroes

1. **REAL TALK** Watch or listen to the teenagers. Match the role models with the reasons.

   1. Usain Bolt ___
   2. big sister ___
   3. Anne Hathaway ___
   4. grandfather ___
   5. a school friend ___
   6. history teacher ___

   a. saved his sister from a fire
   b. helps children
   c. teaches well
   d. is the fastest runner in the world
   e. is nice, smart, and hardworking
   f. dances well

2. **YOUR TURN** Who is *your* role model and why? Tell your partner.

3. Listen to Darren and Lydia talking about heroes. Complete the conversation.

USEFUL LANGUAGE: Asking for and giving clarification

Are you saying that | What do you mean? | What I'm trying to say is that | I mean

Darren: We talked about heroes in class today.
Lydia: That's interesting.
Darren: Yeah, but I didn't agree with most of the people in the class.
Lydia: Really? ¹_____
Darren: Most people chose **movie stars**. I don't think they're heroes.
Lydia: ²_____ celebrities can't be heroes?
Darren: Well, they can be, but maybe they shouldn't be. ³_____, **acting** isn't heroic.
Lydia: But a lot of **movie stars** help people.
Darren: Yes, but most celebrities help people *after* they're famous. ⁴_____ I think everyday people are more heroic.
Lydia: Oh, I see. So, who is your hero?
Darren: **My Aunt Karin. She started a rescue center for wild animals.**
Lydia: Well, that is pretty heroic!

4. Practice the conversation with a partner.

5. **YOUR TURN** Repeat the conversation in Exercise 3, but change the words in purple. Use the information in the chart for one conversation and your own ideas for another.

		My ideas
Type of hero the class chose	pop star	
Activity	singing	
Darren's/your hero	grandfather	
Reason	He fights for peace.	

38 | Unit 4

MY HERO
by Gloria Marconi

My hero is **Captain Sullenberger**. He is famous because he saved the lives of many people. In 2009, he was the pilot on a flight from **New York City**. The airplane engines stopped working. Captain Sullenberger stayed calm and landed the plane in the **Hudson River**. After 2009, he wrote two books about being brave.

I admire Captain Sullenberger due to his heroic act. I also admire him because he is serious about safety. Now he is a **safety expert**, and he gives people and companies advice about being safe. He's also kind and teaches children about aviation and safety. Since he's a good role model, he is my **hero**!

Reading to write: Gloria's hero

6. Look at the photos in Gloria's text. What job does her hero have? Why is he a hero? Read the description to check.

> ### Focus on CONTENT
> When you write about someone you admire, include this information:
> - who he/she is and his/her job
> - heroic things he/she did or does
> - his/her personality
> - why you admire him/her

7. Read Gloria's description again. What information from the Focus on Content box does she include?

> ### Focus on LANGUAGE
> **Connectors to show reasons: *because, since, due to***
> Use a subject and a verb after *because* and *since*. The clause with *because* or *since* can be at the beginning or end of a sentence.
> *I admire my mother **because** she works very hard.*
> ***Since** my aunt helps animals, she's my role model.*
> Use a noun after *due to*. The clause with *due to* can be at the beginning or end of a sentence.
> *Nelson Mandela was famous **due to** his fight for peace.*
> ***Due to** his fight for peace, Nelson Mandela was famous.*

8. Find examples of *because*, *since*, and *due to* in Gloria's description.

9. Circle the correct word or phrase.
1. My cousin Lou was Player of the Year **because / due to** his skills.
2. **Because / Due to** Jenny is kind, we admire her.
3. Painters Frida Kahlo and Diego Rivera were even more famous **since / due to** they were married to each other.
4. J. K. Rowling is a well-known writer **since / due to** her Harry Potter series.

Writing: Your hero

PLAN
First, choose a person you admire. It can be a famous person or someone you know. Use the categories in the Focus on Content box and take notes.

Who he/she is and his/her job	
Heroic things he/she did or does	
His/Her personality	
Why you admire him/her	

WRITE
Now, write about the person you admire. Use your notes to help you. Write at least 60 words.

CHECK
Check your writing. Can you answer "yes" to these questions?
- Is information for each category from the Focus on Content box in your description?
- Do you use connectors to show reasons correctly?

Workbook, pp. 26–27

The Island of CHAMPIONS

Only about three million people live in Jamaica, a small Caribbean island, but many famous athletes are from this country. Athletics is an important part of life in Jamaica, and its athletes are national heroes. Most elementary schools have sports programs, and many high school students compete in an athletics championship, or "Champs," in Kingston every year. Many of the schoolchildren are Olympic champions of the future.

Jamaica's first Olympic heroes were Arthur Wint and Herb McKenley. They won gold and silver medals in the men's 400m race in 1948. From that moment, Jamaican athletics became a national obsession. In 1980, at the Moscow Olympics, Merlene Ottey became the first Jamaican woman to win a medal. She won bronze in the 200m race. She won eight more Olympic medals over 20 years, including two in the 2000 Sydney Olympics at age 40!

In 2008, in Beijing, a new hero won the men's 100m and 200m Olympic gold medals: Usain Bolt. In the London Olympics, in 2012, he became the first athlete to win the "double-double" when he won gold medals in both races again. Jamaican Yohan Blake won silver in both of those races. Shelly-Ann Fraser-Pryce won the gold in the women's 100m and silver in the 200m, bringing home two more medals for Team Jamaica. In fact, Jamaica dominated the medals list in the 2012 Olympics. They won 12 medals, all in track and field events. Jamaica really is the home of champions!

Culture: Athletes from Jamaica

1. Look at the photos. Which country do you think the article is about? Do you know who the runners are?

2. Read and listen to the article. Circle the main idea.
   a. Jamaican high school students are heroes.
   b. Jamaican men and women are equally good at athletics.
   c. There are many Olympic champions from Jamaica.

3. Read the article again. Are the sentences true or false? Write T (true), F (false), or NI (no information).
   1. Jamaica is unusual because it's small, but many athletic champions are from there. ___
   2. Arthur Wint and Herb McKenley were the only Jamaican athletes to win a medal in the 1948 Olympics. ___
   3. Merlene Ottey's first Olympic medal was gold. ___
   4. Usain Bolt won both the 100m and 200m races in Beijing and London. ___

4. **YOUR TURN** Work with a partner. Make a list of famous athletes from your country. Why do people admire them?

   > Lorena Ochoa is famous because she was one of the top female golfers in the world.

   > Yes, and people admire her because she started a golfing school for people in Mexico.

DID YOU KNOW…?
Over 30,000 people go to "Champs" to watch the athletes. Many young runners break national records at the championship.

BE CURIOUS Find out about a mine accident and rescue. How many people were in the mine? (Workbook, p. 79)

Discovery EDUCATION
4.3 THE CHILEAN MINE RESCUE

UNIT 4 REVIEW

Vocabulary

1. **Label the pictures with the correct jobs.**

   1. _____
   2. _____
   3. _____
   4. _____

2. **Complete the sentences with the correct adjectives.**

   | cheerful | funny | serious | kind |

   1. My brother isn't good at telling jokes. He's not very _____.
   2. Martin is always telling jokes. He's not very _____.
   3. Jacquelyn doesn't smile or laugh very often. She's not very _____.
   4. Liz and Josh help kids with their homework after school. They're very _____.

Grammar

3. **Circle the correct words.**

   1. Where **were / did** you last weekend?
   2. **Were / Did** you play sports in high school?
   3. **Was / Did** Mike a fast runner as a child?
   4. **Were / Did** your parents at home last night?

4. **Complete the sentences with the simple past. Then rewrite the sentences with the correct time periods and *ago*.**

   1. I _had_ (have) lunch at 1:00 p.m. Now it's 2:00 p.m.

      I had lunch an hour ago.

   2. Jack _____ (start) school on Monday. Today is Thursday.

      _____

   3. I _____ (call) you at 9:15 a.m. Now it's 9:20 a.m.

      _____

   4. Marcos _____ (be) Most Valuable Player in March. Now it's April.

      _____

Useful language

5. **Complete the conversations with the correct phrases.**

   | Are you saying that | I mean |
   | What do you mean? | What I'm trying to say is that |

   Kim: I think athletes are overpaid.
   Todd: 1_____
   Kim: 2_____, they make too much money.

   Luke: My brother is the fastest runner in the world!
   Sara: 3_____ he runs faster than Usain Bolt?
   Luke: No. 4_____ he runs really fast!

PROGRESS CHECK: Now I can . . .
- ☐ identify some cool jobs.
- ☐ share facts about someone's life.
- ☐ ask and answer questions about being brave.
- ☐ ask for and give clarification.
- ☐ write a description of someone I admire.
- ☐ talk about famous athletes from my country.

REVIEW UNITS 3–4, Workbook, pp. 28–29

CLIL PROJECT
4.4 Amelia Earhart: Famous Flyer, p. 117

5 It's a Mystery!

Discovery EDUCATION

BE CURIOUS

- Mysteries in the Mountains
- What's an unusual or interesting thing that happened to you recently?
- The Case of the Missing Woman
- An Underwater Mystery

1. Who do you think made these statues on Easter Island?
2. Why do you think people made them?
3. Do you know of any mysterious things or places? Where are they?

UNIT CONTENTS

Vocabulary Action verbs; adverbs of manner
Grammar Past continuous; adverbs of time; simple past vs. past continuous; *when* and *while*
Listening I saw something strange last night.

Vocabulary: Action verbs

1. Look at the pictures of a police officer's story.
   Match the sentences with the pictures.

   a. I **caught** the thief after he fell.
   b. I **chased** the thief down the street.
   c. The thief **climbed** the wall.
   d. The thief **hid** the bag.
   e. The thief **fell** on the ground.
   f. The thief **jumped** into someone's yard.
   ✓ g. The thief **stole** a bag and **ran** by my police car.
   h. The thief **threw** the bag over a wall.

2. Listen, check, and repeat.

3. Work with a partner. One person is a reporter and the other is the police officer. Ask and answer questions for each event in the story in Exercise 1.

   What did the thief steal?
   He stole a bag.

   Where did he run?
   He ran by my . . .

Speaking: What can you . . . ?

4. **YOUR TURN** Work with a partner. Think of as many answers as you can for each question. Make a list.

   What can you . . .

   1. catch?   2. chase?   3. climb?   4. hide?   5. jump over?   6. throw?

   catch – a thief, a basketball, a baseball, a bus, a cold . . .

5. Join another pair. Compare your lists.

   Workbook, p. 30

Reading Whodunit?; An Urban Legend; The World's Number One Detective
Conversation Telling and reacting to a story
Writing A narrative about an interesting or unusual event

Unit 5 | 43

Solving MYSTERIES

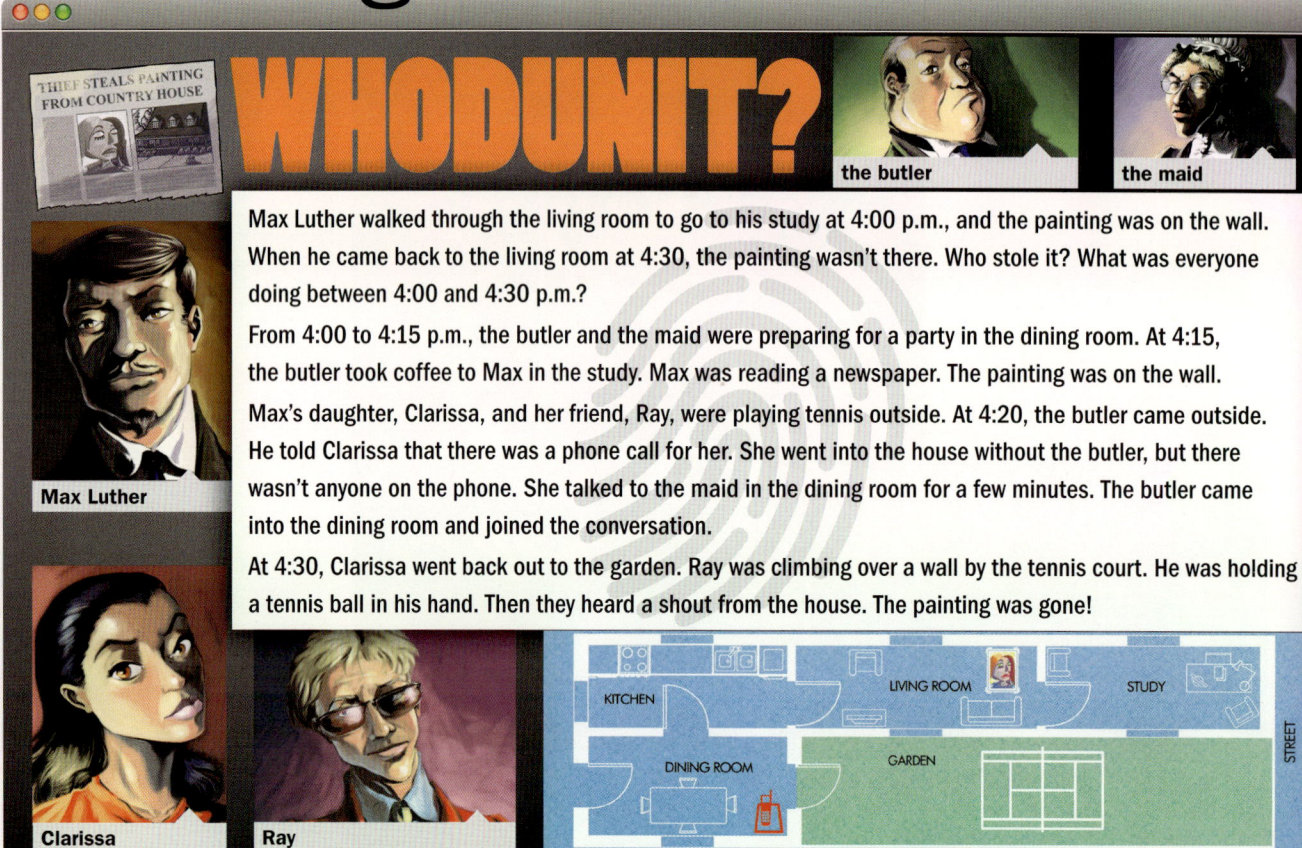

WHODUNIT?

the butler

the maid

Max Luther walked through the living room to go to his study at 4:00 p.m., and the painting was on the wall. When he came back to the living room at 4:30, the painting wasn't there. Who stole it? What was everyone doing between 4:00 and 4:30 p.m.?

From 4:00 to 4:15 p.m., the butler and the maid were preparing for a party in the dining room. At 4:15, the butler took coffee to Max in the study. Max was reading a newspaper. The painting was on the wall.

Max's daughter, Clarissa, and her friend, Ray, were playing tennis outside. At 4:20, the butler came outside. He told Clarissa that there was a phone call for her. She went into the house without the butler, but there wasn't anyone on the phone. She talked to the maid in the dining room for a few minutes. The butler came into the dining room and joined the conversation.

At 4:30, Clarissa went back out to the garden. Ray was climbing over a wall by the tennis court. He was holding a tennis ball in his hand. Then they heard a shout from the house. The painting was gone!

Max Luther

Clarissa

Ray

Reading: An article about a stolen painting

1. **Look at the pictures. What was the crime? Where did it happen?**

2. **Read and listen to the crime story. Who do you think stole the painting? How do you think it happened?**

3. **Read the article again and answer the questions.**

   1. Where was the painting?
      _____

   2. What time did the painting disappear?
      _____

   3. Why were the butler and maid in the dining room?
      _____

   4. Why did Clarissa go into the house?
      _____

   5. What did Ray lose behind the wall?
      _____

4. **Work with a partner. Who stole the painting? Explain your idea. Then check your idea on page 121.**

5. **YOUR TURN** Work with a small group. Do you know any other stories about a thief (real or fictional)? What did the thief steal? Did the police catch him or her?

   > There was a famous bank robbery last year. The thief stole $500,000. The police . . .

DID YOU KNOW...?
Whodunit is an informal word for *Who did it?* People use it to describe crime stories with a mystery.

Grammar: Past continuous

6. Complete the chart.

Use the past continuous to talk about activities that were in progress in the past.		
Wh- questions	**Affirmative answers**	**Negative answers**
What _____ you **doing**?	I **was talking** on the phone.	I **wasn't talking** to Max.
What **was** Max **reading**?	He **was reading** a newspaper.	He _____ **reading** a book.
What **were** they **doing**?	They _____ **playing** tennis.	They **weren't playing** soccer.
Yes/No questions	**Short answers**	
Were you **talking** to Max?	Yes, I **was**.	No, I **wasn't**.
Was Max **reading**?	Yes, he _____.	No, he **wasn't**.
_____ they **playing** tennis?	Yes, they **were**.	No, they _____.

> Check your answers: Grammar reference, p. 110

7. Complete the police report with the past continuous.

POLICE REPORT   CASE NO: 76543

Police officer: Alfred Baker   Name of witness: Jim Hanson   Crime: Stolen bike

Q: What ¹___were___ you ___doing___ (do) at the time?
A: My friends and I ²_____ (play) in the park. I ³_____ (stand) on a hill. From there, I saw the thief steal the bike.
Q: What ⁴_____ the thief _____ (wear)?
A: He ⁵_____ (wear) a blue jacket and jeans.
Q: ⁶_____ your friends _____ (watch) the thief?
A: No, they ⁷_____. They ⁸_____ (ride) their skateboards. They didn't see him.

8. Put the words in the correct order to make questions. Then answer the questions with your own information.

yesterday at 8:00 a.m. / you / what / were / doing
1. *What were you doing yesterday at 8:00 a.m.?*
2. *I was _____*

doing / were / last Saturday at 2:00 p.m. / your friends / what
3. _____
4. _____

Adverbs of time

Use adverbs of time to say when things happened or were happening at a specific time in the past.

this morning/afternoon; yesterday
last night/Monday/weekend/week/month/year
at 2:00 p.m./4:00 p.m./10:00 p.m.

Say it RIGHT! (5.03)

In the word **was**, the **a** makes the short /u/ sound, and the **s** makes the /z/ sound. Listen to the sentences. *What **was** she doing yesterday afternoon? She **was** playing tennis.* Pay attention to your pronunciation of **was** in Exercise 8.

Speaking: What were you doing?

9. YOUR TURN Work with a partner. Think of something you were doing at one of these times. Give your partner clues. Your partner guesses.

yesterday at 12:00 p.m.   last night
last Saturday afternoon   last Friday at 2:00 p.m.

- I was sitting in a stadium and watching something last Saturday afternoon.
- Were you watching a soccer game?
- Yes, I was.

BE CURIOUS — Find out about an archeological dig in Bolivia. What did Scotty and his team find out about the bones? (Workbook, p. 80)

Discovery EDUCATION
5.1 MYSTERIES IN THE MOUNTAINS

Unsolved MYSTERIES

Listening: I saw something strange last night.

1. Did you see or read about something you couldn't explain in the past? What was it?

2. Listen to Kati tell Todd about an unexplained event. What did she see?

3. Listen again. Who did it? Write *K* for Kati or *T* for Todd.

   1. was at home last night _____
   2. was watching TV last night _____
   3. was studying last night _____
   4. is going to watch the sky tonight _____

Vocabulary: Adverbs of manner

4. Look at the pictures and the boldfaced words. These words are adverbs. You can form adverbs from adjectives. Complete the sentences with the correct adverbs. Then listen and check your answers.

quick → **quickly**	bad → **badly**
slow → **slowly**	happy → **happily**
loud → **loudly**	terrible → **terribly** ✓
quiet → **quietly**	hard → **hard**
careful → **carefully**	good → **well**

Spell it RIGHT!

To change an adjective to an adverb:
- change **-y** to **-i** and add **-ly**:
  happy → happ**ily**
- change **-ble** to **-bly**:
  terribl**e** → terrib**ly**

1. Gina slept ___*terribly*___ last night.
2. The dog barked _____.
3. The snail was moving _____.
4. The archaeologist worked with the bones _____.
5. Richard plays the piano _____.
6. The plane flew by _____.
7. Carlos sings _____.
8. The children were playing _____.
9. We entered the room _____.

5. **YOUR TURN** Work with a partner. Ask and answer questions using the adverbs in Exercise 4. Use the words below or your own ideas.

☐ catch a ball	☐ clean your bedroom	☐ play tennis	☐ sing
☐ check your homework	☐ cook	☐ run	☐ throw a ball

Do you run quickly?

No, I don't. I run slowly.

46 | Unit 5

Grammar: Simple past vs. past continuous; *when* and *while*

6. Complete the chart.

> Use the past continuous for an event that was in progress.
> Use the simple past for an event that interrupted the event in progress.
> Use *when* or *while* with the phrase in the past continuous.
> Use *when* with the phrase in the simple past.
>
> I _____ **studying when** I **saw** red lights in the sky.
> (event in progress)   (event that interrupts)
>
> **While/When** I **was studying**, I _____ red lights in the sky.
> (event in progress)   (event that interrupts)
>
> **When** it **happened**, my parents _____ **sleeping**.
> (event that interrupts)   (event in progress)
>
> It _____ **while/when** my parents **were sleeping**.
> (event that interrupts)   (event in progress)

> Check your answers: Grammar reference, p. 110

7. Circle *when* or *while*. Sometimes both answers are possible.

1. Karl caught the ball **(when)** / **(while)** Sandra was running.
2. Olivia was practicing the piano **when** / **while** the phone rang.
3. I heard the loud sound **when** / **while** I was cleaning my room.
4. **When** / **While** the police officer was chasing the thief, he fell.
5. **When** / **While** someone knocked on the door, I was watching TV.

8. Complete the sentences with the simple past or past continuous.

1. Janet watched a mystery movie while she _was eating_ (eat) dinner.
2. I was running in the park when I _____ (see) a police officer.
3. When the lights _____ (go) out, Doug was working.
4. When the fire alarm rang, you _____ (take) a test.
5. While the cat _____ (hide) under the bed, we heard her meow.

Speaking: While you were . . .

9. **YOUR TURN** Work with a partner. Talk about things that happened while you were doing some of these things in the past.

> cooking   eating   exercising   sleeping   studying

> My phone rang while I was sleeping last night.

> Really? When I was sleeping, I had a nightmare.

10. **YOUR TURN** Join another pair. Tell the pair two things that happened to your partner.

> Last night, Jake had a nightmare while he was sleeping.

Get it RIGHT!

Use the simple past, not the past continuous, for an event that interrupts an event in progress.
*Our team was playing well when I **scored** a goal.*
NOT: ~~Our team was playing well when I was scoring a goal.~~

NOTICE IT
A *nightmare* is a very bad dream.

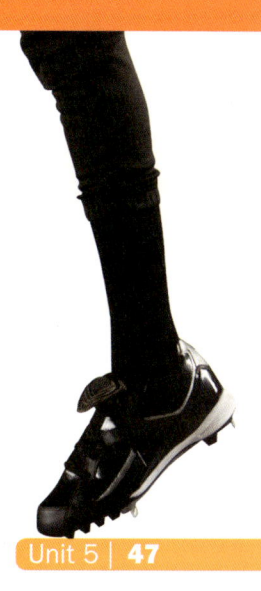

Workbook, pp. 32–33

REAL TALK 5.2 WHAT'S AN UNUSUAL OR INTERESTING THING THAT HAPPENED TO YOU RECENTLY?

Strange STORIES

Conversation: An unusual dream

1. Watch or listen to the teenagers. Circle the correct words.
   1. The boy's soccer team **won** / **lost** the game.
   2. The girl's cat **chased** / **ran toward** her.
   3. **The girl** / **The teacher** gave the class some chocolate for her birthday.
   4. Two girls **wore** / **gave each other** the same shirt.
   5. Someone **made** / **took** the boy's lunch at school.
   6. Someone stole the boy's **bike** / **lock**.

2. **YOUR TURN** What's an unusual or interesting thing that happened to *you* recently? Tell your partner.

3. Dave is telling Anna about a nightmare. Listen and complete the conversation with the words from the box.

USEFUL LANGUAGE: Telling and reacting to a story

| then what happened | Did I tell you about | That's weird! | In the beginning |

Dave: ¹_____ my dream last night?
Anna: No. Tell me about it.
Dave: OK. ²_____, I was **in a park** at night. I was **walking slowly** when a **bear** jumped out at me!
Anna: Oh, no! What did you do?
Dave: I hid behind **a big tree**, and I waited quietly. But **the tree** got smaller and smaller!
Anna: ³_____
Dave: I know. Then the **bear** found me and chased me! While the **bear** was chasing me, I **screamed loudly**!
Anna: So, ⁴_____?
Dave: The **bear** caught me, and I woke up! It was scary!

4. Practice the conversation with a partner.

5. **YOUR TURN** Repeat the conversation in Exercise 3, but change the words in purple. Use the information in the chart for one conversation and your own ideas for another.

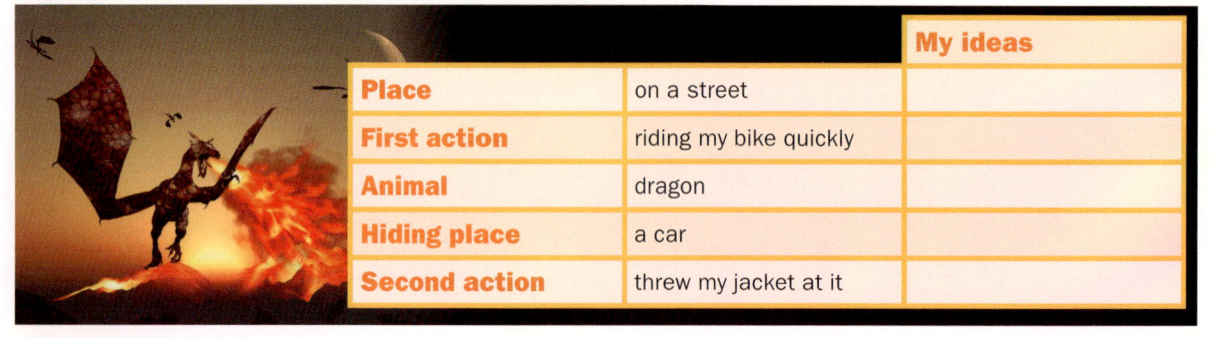

		My ideas
Place	on a street	
First action	riding my bike quickly	
Animal	dragon	
Hiding place	a car	
Second action	threw my jacket at it	

AN URBAN LEGEND
by Stacy Meyers

"Oh, no! I have to help," thought Mickey. One day last summer, he was driving slowly along a quiet road when he saw a car next to the road. A man had a flat tire, and he was trying to change it. Mickey stopped his car and helped the man. While they were changing the tire, they talked about their families. Then the man asked Mickey for his address. At first, Mickey said no, but the man asked him again and again, so Mickey gave it to him. One week later, Mickey got a letter:

> *Dear Mickey,*
> *Thanks for your help. I know a lot about computers but nothing about cars!*
> *Bill Gates*

Finally, Mickey knew who the man was – the founder of one of the world's largest computer companies. He was also one of the richest people in the world. And there was a check for $10,000 with the letter!

Reading to write: A narrative about an unusual event

6. Look at the illustration. What do you think happened? Read Stacy's story to check.

Focus on CONTENT
When you write a story, include:
- a beginning: It should get the readers' attention and make them want to read more.
- a middle: It has details about the events and is in chronological order.
- an ending: It brings the story to a close. A story can have a surprise ending.

7. Read Stacy's story again. What gets the readers' attention at the beginning? What is the surprise ending?

Focus on LANGUAGE
Sequencing words
Use sequencing words to:
- start a story: *One day/night/time, . . . In the beginning, . . .*
- order events: *At first, . . .   Next, . . .   Then . . .*
                After that, . . .   Ten minutes later, . . .
- end a story: *In the end, . . .   Finally, . . .*

8. Find examples of sequencing words in Stacy's story.

9. Complete the story with the correct words.

| at first | finally | later | one night | then |

¹_____, I was doing my homework quietly in my bedroom when I heard a strange noise outside. ²_____, I didn't want to go outside, but ³_____ I opened the door, and I went into the yard. There was a very small dog, and it was barking loudly. While I was playing with the dog, my mom came home. She was laughing. Five minutes ⁴_____, my dad and sister arrived. They were laughing, too. ⁵_____, I understood. The dog was my birthday present!

Writing: Your narrative

PLAN
Think of an interesting or unusual story. It can be something that really happened, or you can create the story. Write notes about the events in the order they happened.

Beginning: _____

Middle: _____
_____
_____
_____

Ending: _____

WRITE
Write your story. Use your notes to help you. Write at least 80 words.

CHECK
Check your writing. Can you answer "yes" to these questions?

- Does your story have a beginning, a middle, and an ending? Are the events in chronological order?
- Do you use sequencing words correctly?

Workbook, pp. 34–35

The World's Number One DETECTIVE

A Sherlock Holmes is famous for solving impossible crimes carefully and easily. He lived at 221B Baker Street in London. He played the violin well and was good at science. He didn't really exist, but he became famous in England more than 125 years ago, and he's famous all over the world today.

B Scottish writer Sir Arthur Conan Doyle wrote the original Sherlock Holmes stories. The first story appeared in a British magazine in 1887. It was the first of 56 stories. Doyle also wrote four Sherlock Holmes books. Doyle was working as a doctor when he wrote the first stories. He often wrote the stories while he was waiting for his patients.

C The detective's assistant, Dr. Watson, is almost as famous as Holmes, and the two always worked together. Holmes liked to explain the crimes to Watson. In the movies, Holmes answers Watson's questions with the phrase, "Elementary, my dear Watson, elementary," which means, "The answer is easy." But Holmes never really said this in any of the original stories or books.

D There are more than 200 Sherlock Holmes movies and TV shows with many different actors playing the roles of Holmes and Watson. In a recent TV series, *Elementary*, the stories take place today. Holmes lives in New York City, and his assistant, Dr. Watson, is a woman.

E Sherlock Holmes is everywhere! There are Sherlock Holmes games, toys, hats, comic books, and video games. There's even a Sherlock Holmes social networking page!

Culture: Sherlock Holmes

1. **Look at the photos. What do you know about Sherlock Holmes? What can you tell about him from the photos?**

2. **Read and listen to the article. Match the paragraphs (A–E) to the topics.**

   1. Holmes in Today's Culture ___
   2. Partners in Crime ___
   3. Holmes in Movies and on TV ___
   4. Fame: Past and Present ___
   5. Sherlock Holmes Stories ___

3. **Read the article again. Circle the correct answers.**

   1. Sherlock Holmes was **a real** / **an imaginary** detective.
   2. The writer of Sherlock Holmes was a **doctor** / **detective**.
   3. In the **movies** / **books**, Holmes's famous phrase is "Elementary, my dear Watson, elementary."
   4. There are about **125** / **200** Sherlock Holmes movies and TV shows.

4. **YOUR TURN** **Work with a partner. Are there any famous fictional characters in your country? Who are they and what do they do?**

   > Pascualina is a famous fictional character. There are many books about her. She travels around the world and . . .

DID YOU KNOW...?

Sherlock Holmes died in one of Doyle's stories in 1893, but the writer brought him back to life because his fans got angry!

BE CURIOUS

Find out about a young woman who disappears from her home. What happened to her? (Workbook, p. 81)

Discovery EDUCATION

5.3 THE CASE OF THE MISSING WOMAN

UNIT 5 REVIEW

Vocabulary

1. **Match the phrases to make sentences.**

   1. A police officer chased the thief ___
   2. The thief threw ___
   3. Then he jumped ___
   4. The thief hid ___

   a. his bag into the river.
   b. at his friend's house until the police officer finally found him.
   c. into the river and swam away.
   d. down the street for 2 kilometers.

2. **Complete the sentences with the correct adverbs of manner.**

   1. Carlos slept _____ (terrible) because of the storm.
   2. My brother sat _____ (quiet) and watched his favorite Sherlock Holmes movie.
   3. The detective studied the crime scene _____ (careful).
   4. He worked _____ (hard) to solve the crime.

Grammar

3. **Look at Gabe's calendar. Write sentences in the past continuous about what he was doing.**

   Monday
   1 8:00 p.m. shop for mom's birthday present

   Wednesday
   3 4:00 p.m. watch a soccer game with brother

   Friday
   12 8:00 a.m – 4:00 p.m. clean the garage
   8:00 p.m. hang out at a café with friend

   1. (last Monday night) _____

   2. (last Wednesday afternoon) _____

   3. (Friday evening) _____

4. **Write sentences using the simple past and past continuous.**

   1. he / answer / the phone / while / he / eat / dinner

   2. we / have / a picnic / when / it / start / to rain

   3. Mark / not wear / a helmet / when / he / fall / off his bike

Useful language

5. **Complete the conversation with the correct phrases.**

   | then what happened | Did I tell you about | That's weird. | In the beginning |

   Elsa: Hey, Ned. ¹_____ my vacation?
   Ned: No, you didn't. Did you have a good time?
   Elsa: ²_____, I had a great time. But then my bag was stolen at a restaurant.
   Ned: Oh, no!
   Elsa: Oh, yes! I put my bag on the back of my chair while I was eating. I didn't even see it happen.
   Ned: ³_____
   Elsa: I know. Luckily, a police officer was sitting next to me. She saw and chased the thief!
   Ned: So, ⁴_____?
   Elsa: She caught the thief and gave me back my bag!

PROGRESS CHECK: Now I can . . .
- ☐ tell a story with action verbs.
- ☐ talk about what I was doing in the past.
- ☐ talk about past events and describe how I do things.
- ☐ tell an interesting or unusual story.
- ☐ write a story about an interesting or unusual event.
- ☐ understand information and talk about fictional characters.

CLIL PROJECT

5.4 An Underwater Mystery, p. 118

Uncover Your Knowledge

UNITS 1–5 Review Game

TEAM 1
START

- In one minute, name a modern example and a traditional example of something for each of these categories: food, music, and sports.

- Ask a teammate about someone he or she knows. Ask two *Wh-* questions and two *Yes/No* questions. Your teammate answers.

- Talk with a teammate about traditions in your families, such as birthdays or weddings. See how long you can keep the conversation going by asking and answering questions.

- In one minute, name as many types of movies as you can.

- Ask a teammate five questions about people's possessions in the classroom. Use *whose*. Your teammate answers.

- In one minute, name five different characters or actors from five different types of TV shows.

- Make five statements about your movie-watching habits using the adverbs of frequency: *always, usually, often, sometimes,* and *never*.

- Role-play a conversation with a teammate about a sports team or sporting event. Keep the conversation going for two minutes.

- You want to go shopping at the mall. Ask a teammate where to buy three different things. Your teammate answers the questions.

- Look around the room. Tell a teammate five things you see happening right now.

- Ask a teammate for his/her opinion about three different TV shows. Disagree with your teammate's opinions.

INSTRUCTIONS:

- ☐ Make teams and choose game pieces.
- ☐ Put your game pieces on your team's START.
- ☐ Flip a coin to see who goes first.
- ☐ Read the first challenge. Can you do it correctly?

   Yes → Continue to the next challenge.

   No → Lose your turn.

The first team to do all of the challenges wins!

TEAM 2
START

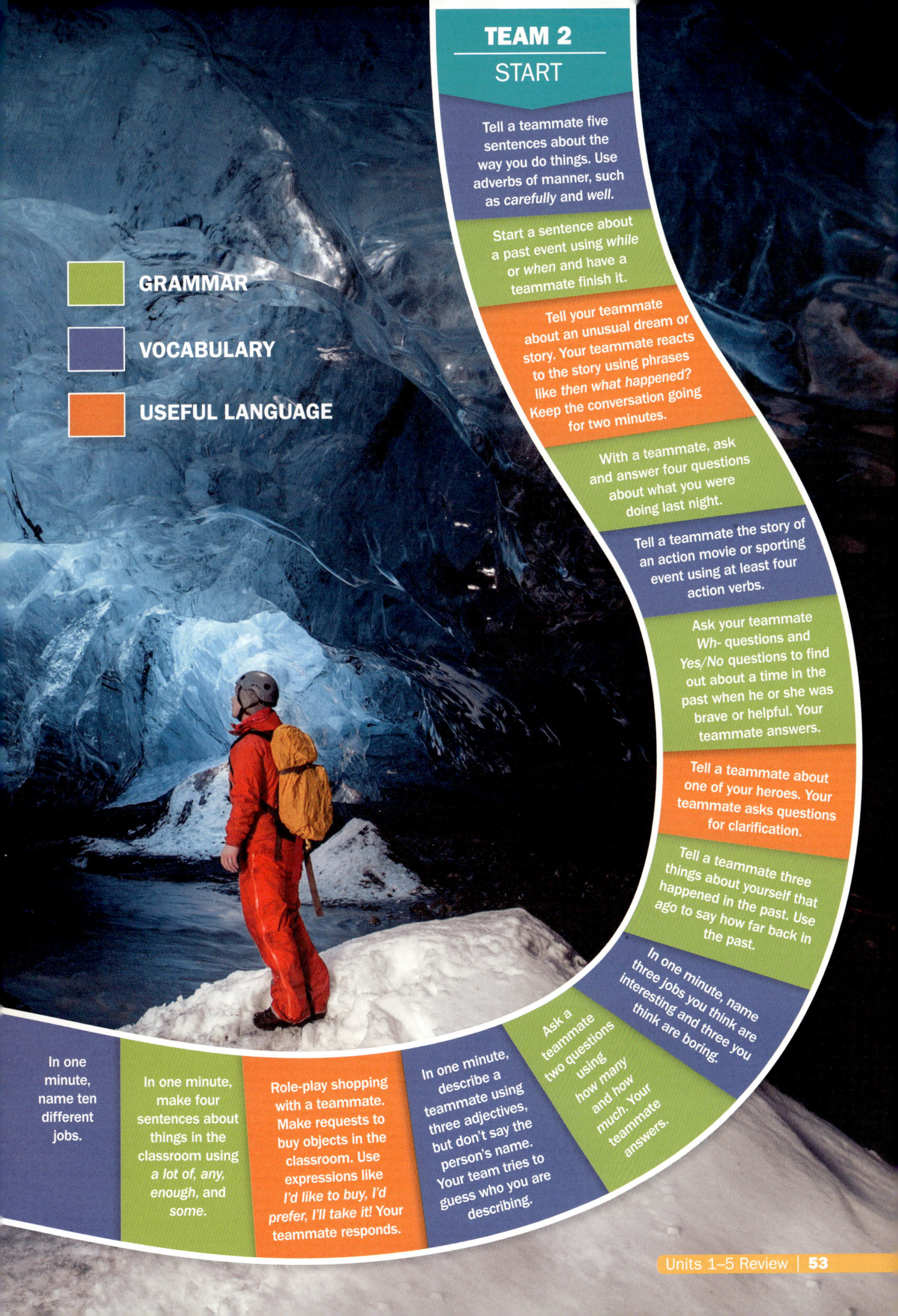

- GRAMMAR
- VOCABULARY
- USEFUL LANGUAGE

1. Tell a teammate five sentences about the way you do things. Use adverbs of manner, such as *carefully* and *well*.

2. Start a sentence about a past event using *while* or *when* and have a teammate finish it.

3. Tell your teammate about an unusual dream or story. Your teammate reacts to the story using phrases like *then what happened?* Keep the conversation going for two minutes.

4. With a teammate, ask and answer four questions about what you were doing last night.

5. Tell a teammate the story of an action movie or sporting event using at least four action verbs.

6. Ask your teammate Wh- questions and Yes/No questions to find out about a time in the past when he or she was brave or helpful. Your teammate answers.

7. Tell a teammate about one of your heroes. Your teammate asks questions for clarification.

8. Tell a teammate three things about yourself that happened in the past. Use *ago* to say how far back in the past.

9. In one minute, name three jobs you think are interesting and three you think are boring.

10. Ask a teammate two questions using *how many* and *how much*. Your teammate answers.

11. In one minute, describe a teammate using three adjectives, but don't say the person's name. Your team tries to guess who you are describing.

12. Role-play shopping with a teammate. Make requests to buy objects in the classroom. Use expressions like *I'd like to buy, I'd prefer, I'll take it!* Your teammate responds.

13. In one minute, make four sentences about things in the classroom using *a lot of, any, enough,* and *some*.

14. In one minute, name ten different jobs.

Units 1–5 Review | 53

Simple present review with be and have, p. 5

Use the simple present of be to identify people and give locations and dates.
Use the simple present of have to talk about possessions, characteristics, and relationships.

be	have
Wh- questions and answers	
Where **am** I? You**'re** in Quito. You**'re not** in Otavalo.	Where **do** I **have** art class? You **have** art in room 9. You **don't have** art in room 10.
Where **are** you? I**'m** in Otavalo. I**'m not** in Quito.	When **do** you **have** art class? I **have** art at 10:00. I **don't have** art at 9:00.
How old **is** he/she/it? He**'s**/She**'s**/It**'s** 14. He**'s**/She**'s**/It**'s not** 17.	What **does** he/she/it **have** for dinner? He/She/It **has** meat. He/She/It **doesn't have** fish.
Who **are** we/they? We/They **are** Maria's parents. We**'re**/They**'re** her grandparents.	What **do** we/they **have**? We/They **have** a computer. We/They **don't have** a desk.
Yes/No questions and answers	
Am I in Quito? Yes, you **are**. / No, you **aren't**.	**Do** I **have** art in room 9? Yes, you **do**. / No, you **don't**.
Are you in Otavalo? Yes, I **am**. / No, I**'m not**.	**Do** you **have** art at 10:00? Yes, I **do**. / No, I **don't**.
Is he/she/it 14? Yes, he/she/it **is**. / No, he/she/it **isn't**.	**Does** he/she/it **have** meat for dinner? Yes, he/she/it **does**. / No, he/she/it **doesn't**.
Are we/they Maria's parents? Yes, we/they **are**. / No, we/they **aren't**.	**Do** we/they **have** a computer? Yes, we/they **do**. / No, we/they **don't**.

1. Complete the sentences with the correct form of be or have. Write affirmative sentences for items with a ✔. Write negative sentences for items with an ✗.

   1. We _____ dinner at 6:00 p.m. (✔)
   2. Lydia _____ 17 years old. (✔)
   3. Dan and Lia _____ a music class. (✗)
   4. You _____ my sister. (✗)
   5. _____ they at school? (✔)
   6. When _____ she _____ lunch? (✔)

whose and possessives, p. 7

Use whose to ask about possession.
Use a name/noun + 's, a possessive adjective, or a possessive pronoun to show possession.

Whose	Possessive 's or s'
Whose computer is it? / **Whose** is it?	It's Dad**'s** computer.
Whose shoes are they? / **Whose** are they?	They're our grandmother**'s** shoes.
Whose house is that? / **Whose** is that?	That's our grandparent**s'** house. That's Lois**'s** house.
Possessive adjectives	**Possessive pronouns**
It's **my/your/his/her/our/their** computer.	It's **mine/yours/his/hers/its/ours/theirs**.
They're **my/your/his/her/our/their** shoes.	They're **mine/yours/his/hers/its/ours/theirs**.
That's **my/your/his/her/its/our/their** house.	That's **mine/yours/his/hers/its/ours/theirs**.

2. Circle the correct words to complete the sentences.

   1. This photo is **my / mine**.
   2. **Who's / Whose** car is that?
   3. I have **Sheila's / hers** pen.
   4. **Yours / Your** phone is small.
   5. That house is **our / ours**.
   6. Look at **their / theirs** faces.

Simple present review, p. 15

Use the simple present to talk about routines, habits, and facts.

Wh- questions	Affirmative answers	Negative answers
What movies **do** you **like**?	I **like** horror movies.	I **don't like** musicals.
How often **does** he/she **go** to the movies?	He/She **goes** to the movies three times a week.	He/She **doesn't go** to the movies on Sundays.
Yes/No questions	**Short answers**	
Do you **like** horror movies?	Yes, I/we **do**.	No, I/we **don't**.
Does he/she **go** to the movies?	Yes, he/she **does**.	No, he/she **doesn't**.
Contractions do not = **don't**	does not = **doesn't**	

1. **Complete the conversation with the simple present.**

    Dan: Hey, Jim. ^{1} _Do_ you _work_ (work) at the movie theater on Elm Street?
    Jim: Yes, I ^{2}_____.
    Dan: ^{3}_____ it _____ (show) animated movies?
    Jim: Yes, it ^{4}_____. There is one there now, *Super Kid*. Why?
    Dan: My brother ^{5}_____ (like) animated movies. Let's all go see it!
    Jim: OK. When?
    Dan: On Sunday. My brother ^{6}_____ (study) in the morning, so let's go at noon.
    Jim: Great. I ^{7}_____ (not work) on Sundays.

Verb + infinitive or *-ing* form (gerund), p. 17

Verb + infinitive	Verb + gerund
have, hope, need, plan, want	dislike, don't mind, enjoy, finish
They **want to watch** a drama.	Sheldon **dislikes trying** new things.
He **needs to see** who gets voted off *Big Brother*.	Leonard **enjoys trying** different things.
I **plan to go** to a movie on Saturday.	We **don't mind watching** commercials.
Verb + infinitive or *-ing* form (gerund)	
hate, like, love, prefer, start	
I **like to read** comic books. I **like reading** comic books.	
They **love to read** comic books. They **love reading** comic books.	
She **hates to watch** reality TV shows. She **hates watching** reality TV shows.	
He **prefers to get** the news online. He **prefers getting** the news online.	

2. **Put the words in the correct order to make sentences. Use the infinitive or gerund form of the underlined word. Sometimes more than one answer is possible.**

    1. about documentaries / <u>read</u> / we / like
       We like to read about documentaries. OR _We like reading about documentaries_.

    2. <u>work</u> / Denny / at 6:00 / finishes
       _____

    3. starts / in the afternoon / it / often / <u>rain</u>
       _____

    4. after school / hopes / <u>watch</u> / her favorite show / Ann
       _____

    5. movies / <u>watch</u> / on my computer / hate / I
       _____

Present continuous review; simple present vs. present continuous, p. 25

Use the present continuous to talk about activities that are happening now.

Wh- questions	Affirmative answers	Negative answers
What **am** I **doing**?	You**'re playing** soccer.	You**'re not playing** baseball.
What **are** you **doing**?	I**'m writing** about my life.	I**'m not writing** about my job.
What **is** he/she **doing**?	He/She **is skating**.	He/She **isn't running**.
What **are** we/they **doing**?	We/They **are watching** the fish.	We/They **aren't skating**.

Yes/No questions	Short answers	
Am I **playing** soccer?	Yes, you **are**.	No, you **aren't**.
Are you **writing** about Dubai?	Yes, I **am**.	No, I**'m not**.
Is he/she **skating**?	Yes, he/she **is**.	No, he/she **isn't**.
Are we/they **shopping**?	Yes, we/they **are**.	No, we/they **aren't**.

Remember: Use the simple present for facts, habits, and routines.

At night, the water **changes** color. = routine
Look! The water **is changing** color. = activity happening now

1. **Circle the correct words to complete the sentences.**
   1. Margot **shop / shops / is shopping / are shopping** in a sporting goods store right now.
   2. Dan and Eduardo **play / plays / is playing / are playing** soccer every Saturday.
   3. Where **do / does / am / are** you usually **go / goes / going / to go** after class?
   4. **Do / Does / Is / Are** she **buy / buys / buying / to buy** a tablet right now?
   5. We **eat / eats / am eating / are eating** at the food court in the mall now.
   6. **Do / Does / Is / Are** Lexi usually **buy / buys / buying / to buy** her books online?

Quantifiers, p. 27

Use quantifiers to show the amount of something.

With countable plural nouns	With uncountable nouns
How **many** T-shirts do you have?	How **much** money do you have?
I have **some / a lot of / enough** T-shirts.	I have **some / a lot of / enough** money.
I **don't** have **many / any / a lot of / enough** T-shirts.	I **don't** have **much / any / a lot of / enough** money.
Are there **many / any / a lot of / enough** T-shirts in your dresser?	Is there **much / any / a lot of / enough** money in your bank account?
Yes, there are. / No, there aren't.	Yes, there is. / No, there isn't.

2. **Circle the correct words to complete the conversation.**

   A: Do you have ¹**many / any** money I can borrow?
   B: Yes, I do. How ²**many / much** money do you need?
   A: I need ³**any / enough** money to buy books for my class.
   B: How ⁴**many / much** books do you need?
   A: I need ⁵**a lot of / much** books! About 10.
   B: Well, how ⁶**many / much** do they cost?
   A: I think about $300 in total.
   B: Oh, OK. Well, I can't lend you $300, but I can lend you ⁷**enough / some** money. It's ⁸**not a lot of / not enough**, but I can lend you $100.
   A: A: That really helps. Thanks! I can pay you back in two weeks.

Simple past statements review and *ago*, p. 35

Use simple past statements to describe things in the past and to talk about past events and activities.
Use ago to say how far back in the past something happened or was.

	Affirmative statements	Negative statements
be	I/He/She **was** MVP in 2011.	I/He/She **wasn't** MVP in 2010.
	They/We/You **were** in Brazil a week **ago**.	They/We/You **weren't** in Spain last week.
Regular verbs	I/He/She/They/We/You **played** for Mexico.	I/He/She/They/We/You **didn't play** for Spain.
	I/He/She/They/We/You **moved** a month **ago**.	I/He/She/They/We/You **didn't move** last week.
Irregular verbs	I/He/She/They/We/You **made** a solo album in 2003.	I/He/She/They/We/You **didn't make** an album in 2001.
	I/He/She/They/We/You **got** a tablet a year **ago**.	I/He/She/They/We/You **didn't get** a laptop.

For regular verbs: + -ed: work → work**ed**   + -d: live → live**d**
                     -y → -i + -ed: try → tri**ed**   double consonant + -ed: shop → shop**ped**

For irregular verbs: See p. 121.

1. Write statements in the simple past.

1. we / win / two medals a year ago   *We won two medals a year ago.*
2. Dennis / grow up / in Guatemala   _____
3. Cassie / be / Player of the Year in 2014   _____
4. my friends / not sing / at the party last night   _____
5. you / be / funny at the party last weekend   _____

Simple past questions review and *ago*, p. 37

Use simple past questions to ask about past things, events, and activities.
Use ago to ask how far back in the past something happened or was.

	Wh- questions and answers	Yes/No questions and answers
be	How **was** he/she an hour **ago**? He/She **was** happy.	**Was** he/she happy an hour **ago**? Yes, he/she **was**. / No, he/she **wasn't**.
	Where **were** they/we? They/We **were** at home.	**Were** they/we/you at home? Yes, they/we/you **were**. / No, they/we/you **weren't**.
Regular verbs	How long **ago did** I/he/she/it/they/we/you **start**? I/He/She/It/They/We/You **started** an hour **ago**.	**Did** I/he/she/it/they/we/you **start** an hour **ago**? Yes, I/he/she/it/they/we/you **did**. / No, I/he/she/it/they/we/you **didn't**.
	Why **did** I/he/she/they/we/you **carry** him? I/He/She/They/We/You **carried** him because he was hurt.	**Did** I/he/she/they/we/you **carry** him? Yes, I/he/she/they/we/you **did**. / No, I/he/she/they/we/you **didn't**.
Irregular verbs	What **did** I/he/she/they/we/you **see**? I **saw** a fire.	**Did** I/he/she/they/we/you **see** a fire? Yes, I/he/she/they/we/you **did**. / No, I/he/she/they/we/you **didn't**.
	Where **did** I/he/she/they/we/you **put** the ladder? I/He/She/They/We/You **put** it against the house.	**Did** I/he/she/they/we/you **put** the ladder against the house? Yes, I/he/she/they/we/you **did**. / No, I/he/she/they/we/you **didn't**.

2. Write questions for the answers.

1. **A:** *Where did you go last night?*   **B:** I went to a soccer game.
2. **A:** _____   **B:** I saw a famous writer at the restaurant.
3. **A:** _____   **B:** No, I wasn't at the concert. I was at home.
4. **A:** _____   **B:** Yes, I did. I studied for two hours last night.
5. **A:** _____   **B:** I wrote about my aunt because I admire her.

Past continuous, p. 45

Use the past continuous to talk about activities that were in progress in the past.

Wh- questions	Affirmative answers	Negative answers
Who **was** I **talking** to?	You **were talking** to the butler.	You **weren't talking** to the maid.
What **were** you **doing**?	I **was talking** on the phone.	I **wasn't talking** to Max.
What **was** he/she **reading**?	He/She **was reading** a newspaper.	He/She **wasn't reading** a book.
What **were** they/we **doing**?	They/We **were playing** tennis.	They/We **weren't playing** soccer.
Yes/No questions	Short answers	
Was I **talking** to the teacher?	Yes, you **were**.	No, you **weren't**.
Were you **talking** to Max?	Yes, I **was**.	No, I **wasn't**.
Was Max **reading**?	Yes, he **was**.	No, he **wasn't**.
Were they **playing** tennis?	Yes, they **were**.	No, they **weren't**.

1. **Complete the questions and answers with the past continuous.**

    1. **A:** What _____ you _____ (do) last night at 9:00 p.m.?

       B: I _____ (listen) to music, but I _____ (not listen) to it loudly.

    2. **A:** _____ Rosa _____ (watch) a detective show this afternoon?

       B: No, she _____. She _____ (clean) her bedroom.

    3. **A:** _____ they _____ (chasing) their dog at 8:00 a.m.?

       B: Yes. They _____ (chase) it in the park, but they _____ (not run) very fast.

    4. **A:** _____ you _____ (study) for the science test yesterday?

       B: Yes, I _____. I _____ (work) with Jorge.

Simple past vs. past continuous; *when* and *while*, p. 47

Use the past continuous for an event that was in progress.
Use the simple past for an event that interrupted the event in progress.
Use when or while with the phrase in the past continuous.
Use when with the phrase in the simple past.

I **was studying** (event in progress)	**when** I **saw** red lights in the sky. (event that interrupts)
While/When I **was studying**, (event in progress)	I **saw** red lights in the sky. (event that interrupts)
When it **happened**, (event that interrupts)	my parents **were sleeping**. (event in progress)
It **happened** (event that interrupts)	**while/when** my parents **were sleeping**. (event in progress)

2. **Circle the correct words to complete the sentences.**

    1. Don **took / was taking** photos when a thief **stole / was stealing** his camera.

    2. The phone **rang / was ringing** while Britney **watched / was watching** TV.

    3. When the detective **entered / was entering** the room, the maid **cleaned / was cleaning** the house.

    4. While I **read / was reading** about Easter Island, someone **knocked / was knocking** on the door.

    5. Someone **screamed / was screaming** loudly when Sara and Maria **walked / were walking** their dog.

This page intentionally left blank.

CLIL PROJECT

ROBOTS in the Real WORLD

1. **Complete the sentences with the correct words.**

   | communicate | computer | create | design | machine | professor | teacher |

   1. A _____ is a higher-level _____ in a university.
   2. A _____ is a thinking _____. It can _____ with other ones.
   3. To _____ something is to make or draw plans for it. Next, you _____ it.

   Discovery EDUCATION
   2.4 WHO'S REAL?

2. **Watch the video. Are the sentences true (*T*) or false (*F*)?**

   1. Professor Ishiguro is wearing a blue shirt. ____
   2. The robot is wearing a watch. ____
   3. Professor Ishiguro's first name is Hitoshi. ____
   4. One of the three students is a woman. ____
   5. They sit at a round table. ____
   6. The white robot can run and turn around. ____

3. **Complete the paragraph with the correct words.**

   | color | glasses | hair | move | same | shy | strange | think | twins |

   Look at these two men. What looks the ¹_____? What looks different? Now look at their faces and look at their ²_____. It's the same ³_____, isn't it? And they both have ⁴_____. So what do you ⁵_____? Are they ⁶_____? OK, now watch how they ⁷_____. What's ⁸_____ here? This man isn't talking. Is he very ⁹_____?

   > **PROJECT**
   >
   > Plan your own robot – what do you want your robot to do? Answer the questions below. Then draw or make a model of your robot. Show your robot to the class and tell them about it.
   >
   > - What three things do you want your robot to do for you?
   > - Do you think you will enjoy life with a robot? Why or why not?
   > - What do you think robots will do in the next few years?
   > - Will robots make life better or worse for people? Why?

Unsolved MYSTERIES

1. **Amelia Earhart was a famous female pilot from the United States. Label the places from Amelia's last flight.**

   | Howland Island | Lae, Papua New Guinea | North Africa | Pacific Ocean | South America | South Asia |

2. **Watch the video. Number the sentences in the order that you hear them from 1–6.**

   ____ a. Next, they went across North Africa and South Asia.

   ____ b. She was one of the first female pilots.

   ____ c. She traveled with a navigator.

   ____ d. We are on the line 157–337.

   ____ e. In 2001, a team looked for clues.

   ____ f. But the island was very small and difficult to find.

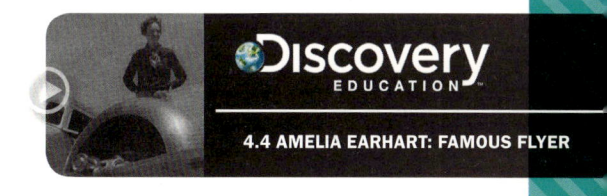

   4.4 AMELIA EARHART: FAMOUS FLYER

PROJECT — Here are some famous mysteries. Choose the most interesting one and find out more about it. Write an explanation of what you think happened.

MYSTERY:	Sailors found the ship *Mary Celeste* abandoned with one lifeboat missing
WHEN:	December 1872
WHERE:	Atlantic Ocean, near Africa
FACTS:	Weather was good, plenty of food and water on ship
WHAT HAPPENED?	

MYSTERY:	Building Stonehenge
WHEN:	3000–2000 BCE
WHERE:	The south of England
FACTS:	Made from stones weighing 45 tons from 40 kilometers away and stones weighing almost 4 tons from 390 kilometers away
WHAT HAPPENED?	

MYSTERY:	The Yeti, a large animal, like an ape
WHEN:	First spotted in the 1800s
WHERE:	The Himalayas, in Nepal and Tibet
FACTS:	Many people believe it exists, but there are no photographs of it.
WHAT HAPPENED?	

Life below the SURFACE

CLIL PROJECT

1. **Label the pictures with the correct words.**

   diver   storyteller   Tokyo   tower   Yonaguni

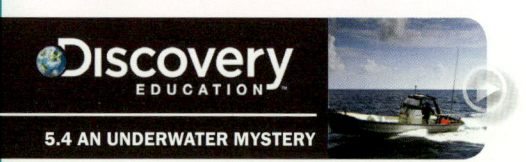

   1 _____   2 _____   3 _____   4 _____   5 _____

   Discovery EDUCATION
   5.4 AN UNDERWATER MYSTERY

2. **Watch the video. Complete the sentences with the correct conjunctions.**

   and   but   so   when

   1. Not many people live on these islands, _____ it's quiet and calm.
   2. Yonaguni is part of Japan, _____ it has its own language and culture.
   3. In the 1980s, he was diving near the island of Yonaguni _____ he found something amazing.
   4. It had streets, steps, _____ tall towers.

3. **Are the sentences true (T) or false (F)?**

   1. Yonaguni is to the north of Japan. ____
   2. About a hundred people live on Yonaguni. ____
   3. The people here tell old stories to their children. ____
   4. Kihachiro Aratake is a driver. ____
   5. It looked like a large city under the water. ____
   6. Some scientists think the structure was once above the water. ____

PROJECT

Do you know the story of the Lost City of Atlantis? Some people believe Atlantis was an underwater city, like the structures around Yonaguni.

Find out more about Atlantis and complete the chart below. Then compare the stories of Atlantis and Yonaguni and make a presentation about these two places.

	Atlantis	**Yonaguni**
Possible location(s)?		*off the coast of Japan*
When did the city exist?		*10,000 years ago*
What do people believe happened to the city?		
What do you believe?		

Uncover 2 Combo A

Lynne M. Robertson

Workbook

CAMBRIDGE UNIVERSITY PRESS

Discovery EDUCATION

1 Traditions

VOCABULARY Categories

1 Write the letters in the correct categories.

a. b.
c. d.
e. f.
g. h.
i. j.
k. l.

1. music ____d____, _____
2. sports _____, _____
3. food _____, _____
4. places _____, _____
5. art _____, _____
6. clothing _____, _____

2 Look at the pictures in Exercise 1. Circle the correct answer.

1. Which one is modern?
   d   f   (e)

2. Which one do people wear today?
   a   b   c

3. Which one is a modern place?
   e   g   h

4. Which one is traditional art?
   a   h   j

5. Which one is traditional?
   e   f   l

3 Complete the sentences with the six category words from Exercise 1.

1. My mother won't listen to modern ____music____.

2. They like modern _____ like photography.

3. He sells jeans and T-shirts in a _____ store.

4. She knows how to cook traditional _____.

5. You can learn traditional _____ like karate.

6. We like to visit traditional _____ with old buildings.

4 Answer the questions with your own information.

1. What kind of music do you like?
   I like dance music.
   Is it traditional or modern?
   ____modern____

2. What food do you like?
   _____
   Is it traditional or modern?
   _____

3. What clothing do you like?
   _____
   Is it traditional or modern?
   _____

4. What sport do you like?
   _____
   Is it traditional or modern?
   _____

GRAMMAR Simple present review with *be* and *have*

1 Circle the correct simple present forms of *be* and *have*.

1. A: Who **is** / **are** you?
   B: I **'s** / **'m** Maya's brother.
2. A: Where **is** / **are** they?
   B: They **'s** / **'re** at the swimming pool.
3. A: What **do** / **does** she **have** / **has**?
   B: She **have** / **has** a laptop. She **don't have** / **doesn't have** a tablet.
4. A: When do they **have** / **has** science?
   B: They **have** / **has** science in the afternoon.
5. A: **Is** / **Are** he good at soccer?
   B: No, he **isn't** / **aren't**.
6. A: **Is** / **Are** we in the same English class?
   B: Yes, we **is** / **are**.
7. A: **Do** / **Does** you **have** / **has** a new bike?
   B: No, I **don't** / **doesn't**.
8. A: **Do** / **Does** she **have** / **has** traditional clothes?
   B: Yes, she **do** / **does**.

2 Match the questions with the correct answers.

1. Are they in the same class? _f_
2. Do you have a bike? ____
3. What's the date today? ____
4. Where are my parents? ____
5. What does he have in his bag? ____
6. Do they have a pet snake? ____

a. They're at the store.
b. He has a tablet. He doesn't have a book.
c. No, they don't. They have a rabbit.
d. It's the 18th.
e. No, I don't. I have a car.
f. Yes, they are.

3 Rewrite the sentences as *Wh-* questions and *yes/no* questions.

1. I am in Ecuador.
   Where are you? / Are you in Ecuador?
2. They are on the football team.
   _____
   _____
3. I have English in the morning.
   _____
   _____
4. She has a new computer.
   _____
   _____
5. He's at the party today.
   _____
   _____
6. They have an old car.
   _____
   _____

4 Complete the questions with *be* or *have*. Then answer the questions with your own information.

1. Where ____*are*____ you now?
   I'm in the library.
2. When do you _____ dinner?
   _____
   _____
3. How old _____ your friend?
   _____
   _____
4. _____ you at the beach now?
   _____
   _____
5. Does your friend _____ a cold?
   _____
   _____
6. _____ it sunny today?
   _____
   _____

VOCABULARY Clothes and objects

1 Put the letters in the correct order to make words.

1. TAH _____hat_____
2. NEP _____
3. EHOSS _____
4. SREDS _____
5. HATCW _____
6. CAKTEJ _____
7. OVEENIITSL _____
8. OPHNEELET _____
9. TPOECMUR _____
10. ROHHATGPOP _____

2 Label the pictures with the correct words from Exercise 1.

1. _____dress_____
2. _____
3. _____
4. _____
5. _____
6. _____
7. _____
8. _____
9. _____
10. _____

3 Circle the correct answers.

1. Which one is a traditional object?
   a. television
   (b.) pen
   c. computer

2. Which one is clothing?
   a. photo
   b. phone
   c. dress

3. Which one do people wear on their feet?
   a. phone
   b. shoes
   c. TV

4. Which one DON'T you use to write?
   a. pen
   b. jacket
   c. computer

5. Which one do you wear on your head?
   a. hat
   b. dress
   c. watch

4 Complete the sentences with the correct words.

| pen | phone | photo | ✓TV | watch |

1. They have a new flat screen _____TV_____.
2. I have an old black-and-white _____ of my great-grandparents.
3. I use a computer to send emails, but my grandfather uses a _____ to write letters.
4. My mother wears a _____, but I use my phone to tell time.
5. My grandmother sent me a text from her new _____.

GRAMMAR *whose* and possessives

1 Circle the correct answers.

1. **Whose** / **Who's** hat is that?
2. **Whose** / **Who's** Alex's sister?
3. **Whose** / **Who's** sister is that?
4. **Whose** / **Who's** are those?
5. **Whose** / **Who's** photos are they?
6. **Whose** / **Who's** on the phone?

2 Complete the chart with the correct possessive adjectives and pronouns.

Possessive adjectives	Possessive pronouns
It's ___my___ phone.	It's mine.
That's your hat.	That hat is _____.
That's _____ photo.	That's hers.
They're his shoes.	They're _____.
They're _____ pens.	They're ours.
It's their TV.	It's _____.

3 Complete the sentences with possessive 's or s'.

1. That's my uncle_'s_ motorcycle.
2. It's my three cousin____ house.
3. That's my grandparent____ computer.
4. They're his mother____ books.
5. It's my parent____ car.
6. They're the school____ cameras.

4 Complete the conversation with *whose* and possessives.

Meg: Are these [1] ___your___ photos from your trip?

Robert: Yes, they are. Look. That's my grandparent[2]_____ house. And that's my grandfather[3]_____ new motorcycle.

Meg: Really?

Robert: Yes, it's [4]_____. Look at this photo.

Meg: [5]_____ bicycles are those?

Robert: They're my cousin[6]_____ bikes.

Meg: [7]_____ riding the skateboard?

Robert: That's my mom. It's [8]_____ skateboard.

Meg: Wow! That's cool.

CONVERSATION — A cool tradition

1 Put the sentences in the correct order to make a conversation.

____ Hiro: Well, we have a party, of course. But my cousins and I have a new tradition.

____ Lena: That's a cool idea!

____ Hiro: It is. We email it to my grandparents, too. They love it.

____ Lena: Really? How do you do that?

____ Hiro: We use family photos.

____ Lena: That's interesting. What is it?

____ Hiro: We go to the computer lab and make a video.

____ Lena: (Tell me about it.)

__1__ Hiro: It's my aunt's birthday on Saturday.

2 Circle the phrases in Exercise 1 that keep the conversation going.

3 Circle the correct answer to keep the conversation going.

1. **A:** Did you know that brides in India paint their hair red?
   B: ⓐ That's interesting.   b. OK.

2. **A:** I think rock stars are cool.
   B: a. I'm sorry to hear that.   b. Really?

3. **A:** My sister works on TV.
   B: a. Tell me about it.   b. How are you?

4. **A:** I'm in the math competition. We go to Chicago on Monday!
   B: a. See you later.   b. Then what?

4 Keep the conversations going with the correct phrases.

| Really? | That's interesting. |
| ✓Tell me about it. | Then what? |

1. **A:** The library has a movie night for teens on Fridays. It's really fun.
   B: *Tell me about it.*

2. **A:** My aunt works at the park. She sees bears a lot.
   B: _____
   A: Yes. There are a lot of bears.

3. **A:** The new mall is open. It has an ice cream shop next to a gym.
   B: _____

4. **A:** There's a band competition in the park on Saturday. My band thinks we can win it.
   B: _____
   A: Then we win some money!

READING TO WRITE

1 Complete the invitation with the correct question words.

Who ✓What Where When Why

Tim's Party!

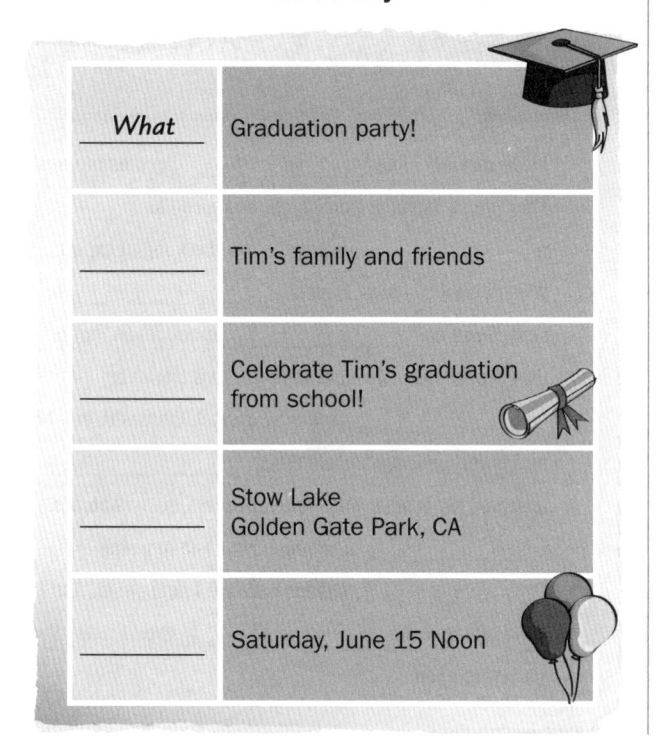

What	Graduation party!
_____	Tim's family and friends
_____	Celebrate Tim's graduation from school!
_____	Stow Lake Golden Gate Park, CA
_____	Saturday, June 15 Noon

2 Complete the word web with information about Tim's party.

cake, music
lots of games, activities
many friends, grandparents, cousins
Saturday noon
✓ the park

3 Circle the correct answers.

1. **There is** / **There are** a lot of people in my family.
2. **There is** / **There are** many interesting traditions in the world.
3. **There is** / **There are** a museum with traditional Asian art on Larkin Street.
4. **There is** / **There are** a new sport called "snow kiting."
5. **There isn't** / **There aren't** a professional women's baseball team.

4 Write sentences about Tim's party. Use the word web from Exercise 2. Use *There is / There are*.

1. _There is a birthday party for Tim in the park._
2. _____
3. _____
4. _____
5. _____

When

Where
the park

Tim's graduation party

Who

What

Unit 1 | 7

2 What's Playing?

VOCABULARY Types of movies

1 Complete the crossword puzzle.

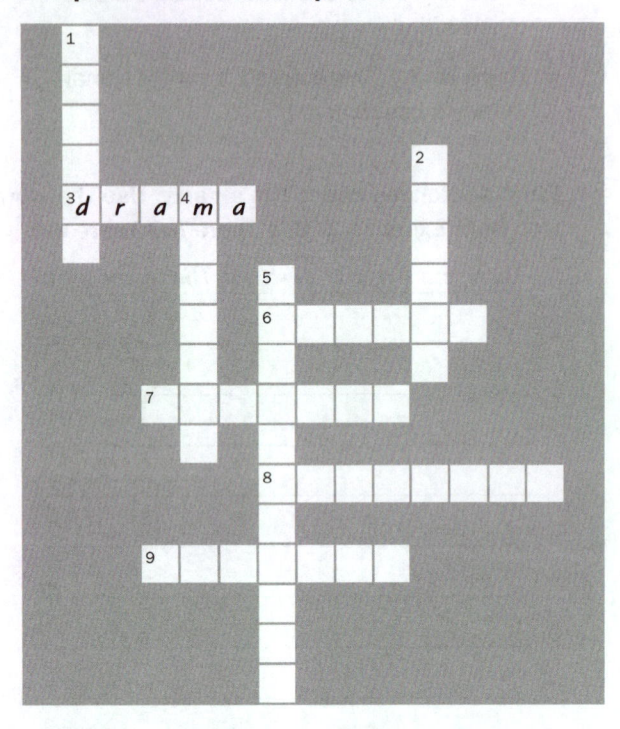

ACROSS   DOWN

3.
6.
7.
8.

1.
2.
4.
5.
9.

2 Complete the paragraph with words from Exercise 1.

My Post

I love movies! I like ¹ __action__ movies the best. They are so exciting. I do karate, so I also like ² _____ movies to see the kung fu experts. When I want to laugh, I watch a ³ _____ or sometimes an ⁴ _____ movie, even though they are for kids. My mom likes the love stories in ⁵ _____ movies so I watch them with her. My dad is very serious, and we watch ⁶ _____ together. My brother likes special effects, so he watches ⁷ _____ movies. I don't like to watch ⁸ _____ movies because I get scared. And I don't like to watch ⁹ _____, even though the singing is good.

Comment

3 Complete the sentences with your own ideas.

1. My favorite type of movie is ____horror movies____ because __I like scary stories_____.

2. The name of my favorite movie is _____.

3. My favorite movie villain is _____ _____ because _____.

4. I don't like _____ movies because _____ _____.

5. I never watch _____ _____.

8 | Unit 2

GRAMMAR Simple present review

1 Match the questions with the correct answers.

1. Do you like action movies? _c_
2. Does Helen like romance movies? ____
3. Do they watch "Bollywood" movies? ____
4. What type of movies do you watch? ____
5. Where do they watch movies? ____
6. How often does Maria go to the movies? ____

a. They watch movies at home.
b. Yes, she does.
c. No, I don't.
d. I watch horror movies.
e. She never goes to the movies.
f. Yes, they do.

2 Complete the chart. Use the simple present.

	Questions	Affirmative	Negative
1. **I**	What movies do you like?	I _like_ musicals.	I _don't like_ dramas.
2. **They**	What ____ they ____ her?	They call her "J.Lo."	They ____ her Jennifer Muñiz.
3. **She**	How often ____ Sally ____ to the movies?	She ____ to the movies two times a week.	She doesn't go to the movies on Fridays.
4. **I**	Do you like documentaries?	Yes, I ____.	No, I ____.
5. **They**	____ they watch movies at school?	____.	____.
6. **He**	____ Owen ____ to the movies?	____.	____.

GRAMMAR Adverbs of frequency

3 Complete the chart with adverbs of frequency.

✓always   never   often   sometimes   usually

always
____
____
____
____

4 Put the words in the correct order to make sentences.

1. watch / at / never / movies / night / horror / I / .
   I never watch horror movies at night.
2. with / I / watch / sisters / my / romance / usually / movies / .
   ____
3. movies / on / her / sometimes / watches / computer / She / .
   ____
4. always / animated / brother / movies / My / on / the / watches / weekends / .
   ____

5 Answer the questions with your own information.

1. How often do you watch movies at school?
   We sometimes watch movies at school.
2. When do you watch movies with your friends?
   ____
3. What types of movies do you never watch?
   ____
4. Where do you usually watch movies?
   ____
5. Do you go to the movie theater? How often?
   ____

Unit 2 | 9

VOCABULARY Types of TV shows

1 Find the words for TV shows.

cartoon	crime series	documentary
game show	reality TV show	sitcom
soap opera	talk show	✓ the news

H	T	H	E	N	E	W	S	O	E	N	U	J
R	E	A	L	I	T	Y	T	V	S	H	O	W
R	P	C	A	R	T	O	O	N	S	T	Y	Z
P	C	R	I	M	E	S	E	R	I	E	S	U
E	Z	V	X	H	I	N	R	Y	Z	R	H	G
O	R	Q	E	B	I	P	N	L	V	K	K	T
M	X	D	O	C	U	M	E	N	T	A	R	Y
R	D	K	W	F	O	M	V	E	L	H	P	M
D	S	I	T	C	O	M	K	U	R	S	R	T
J	S	O	A	P	O	P	E	R	A	N	L	W
J	J	N	S	V	P	Y	O	K	Q	E	S	Q
L	G	A	M	E	S	H	O	W	C	R	P	Y
Z	T	H	I	T	A	L	K	S	H	O	W	K

2 Label the pictures with the correct types of TV shows from Exercise 1.

1. _____reality TV show_____
2. _____
3. _____
4. _____
5. _____
6. _____
7. _____
8. _____
9. _____

3 Write the types of TV shows from Exercise 1.

1. This type of TV show has funny situations that make you laugh. _____sitcom_____
2. You see real events that happen in the world every day on these shows. _____
3. This type of show often has police officers chasing villains. _____
4. In this type of show, people compete to win prizes and money. _____
5. This is usually a serious show that talks about one issue or topic. _____
6. This is an animated TV show, usually made for children. _____
7. You can watch strong characters and stories full of romance and drama in this type of show. _____
8. This show features several people sitting around talking. _____
9. People who aren't actors get into drama or competition in this type of show. _____

4 Choose three people you know. Write sentences about the TV shows they watch.

1. *My parents watch the news.*
2. _____
3. _____
4. _____
5. _____

GRAMMAR Verb + infinitive or -ing form (gerund)

1 Does each sentence have a verb + infinitive or a verb + -ing form (gerund)? Underline verb + infinitive. Circle verb + -ing form.

1. She <u>loves to read</u> comic books. / She (loves reading) comic books.
2. My brother dislikes buying new clothes.
3. Ellen prefers watching movies to reading movie reviews.
4. Henry needs to get money to buy a bike.
5. Mila enjoys watching all types of movies.
6. They want to write a movie script together.

2 Use the phrases to complete the chart with verb + infinitive or verb + -ing form (gerund).

dislikes being	dislikes reading	hates being
hates to be	✓need to see	prefer eating
prefer to eat	wants to go	

Verb + infinitive
You _____need to see_____ this TV show.
Howie _____ to outer space.

Verb + -ing form (gerund)
Sheldon _____ wrong.
Penny _____ comic books.

Verb + infinitive or -ing form (gerund)
Raj _____ shy. / Raj _____ shy.
They _____ Thai food on Monday night. / They _____ Thai food on Monday night.

3 Correct the sentences.

1. I dislike ~~to go~~ *going* to bed late.
2. They enjoy to washing the dog.
3. We need seeing the map.
4. Helen likes study science at school.
5. Hank wants to watching sports on TV.
6. She hates get up late.

4 Write sentences with your own information. Use *love, enjoy, want, prefer, dislike,* and *hate* plus the infinitive or -ing forms of the verbs in the box.

| get | ✓play | read | study | watch | work |

1. (love) *I love to play video games.*
   I love playing video games.
2. (enjoy) _____
3. (dislike) _____
4. (want) _____
5. (hate) _____
6. (prefer) _____

CONVERSATION It's really funny!

1 Put the words in the correct order to make sentences.

1. do / feel / you / How / about / reality TV shows / ?

   How do you feel about reality TV shows?

2. my / In / they're / opinion, / boring / .

   _____

3. about / you / sitcoms / do / think / What / ?

   _____

4. OK / I / they're / think / .

   _____

5. about / you / soap operas / do / How / feel / ?

   _____

2 Put the sentences in the correct order to make a conversation.

____ Paul: Well, I watch for the story, not the acting.

____ Erika: In my opinion, they're really awful. The actors who play the villains are so bad.

____ Paul: I think they're boring. I prefer to read a book.

____ Erika: Oh, well, then what do you think of documentaries?

_1_ Paul: Hey, Erika. What do you think about crime series?

____ Erika: I think they're great. You can learn a lot.

3 Ask for and give opinions. Use the phrases and your own opinions.

| How do you feel about | In my opinion, |
| I think | What do you think about |

1. *How do you feel about* soap operas?

   _____
   _____

2. _____ crime series?

   _____
   _____

3. _____ reality TV shows?

   _____
   _____

4. _____ sitcoms?

   _____
   _____

12 | Unit 2

READING TO WRITE

1 Read Tim's movie review. Then complete the chart.

This review is of Disney's *Maleficent*. It is an action/adventure movie based on the villain from the old fairy tale, "Sleeping Beauty." It has the same director as *The Hunger Games*, Robert Stromberg.

Angelina Jolie stars as Maleficent, a beautiful fairy from a long time ago in a peaceful forest. But one day, a human army invades the forest and threatens the peace. Maleficent becomes a strong leader, but someone betrays her(so)her heart turns to stone. She *curses the human king's new baby, Aurora, to die before she is 16. As the baby grows older, Maleficent learns that Aurora (actor Elle Fanning) may be the key to peace in the forest.

I like this movie because it is a new story about an old villain. Angelina Jolie is beautiful and mysterious as Maleficent, so she makes the character very interesting. The fairy tale really comes to life because the director did a good job with the camerawork and costumes.

*****curse** – to use magical words that make something bad happen

Main characters and actors	Director *Robert Stromberg*
Type of movie	Time and place
Short description of the story	
Why you like it or don't like it	

2 Complete the chart about a movie you like.

Main characters and actors	Director
Type of movie	Time and place
Short description of the story	
Why you like it or don't like it	

3 Circle the examples of the connectors *so* and *because* in Exercise 1. Then use your notes from Exercise 2 to write sentences using *so* and *because*.

1. *I liked this movie because the animation looked very real.*
2. _____
3. _____
4. _____

REVIEW UNITS 1–2

1 Put the words in the correct columns.

| basketball | hip-hop | jazz |
| meat with corn | pizza | sumo wrestling |

Food	Music	Sports

2 Write one traditional thing for each category from Exercise 1.

1. Food: _____
2. Music: _____
3. Sports: _____

3 Complete the questions and answers with the correct forms of *be* or *have*. Then match the questions with the correct answers.

1. What _____ he _____ for lunch? ____
2. How old _____ Ken? ____
3. Do they _____ a tablet? ____
4. _____ they your cousins? ____

a. Yes, they are.
b. He's 15. He _____ 17.
c. He _____ sushi. He doesn't have a burger.
d. No, they don't.

4 Look at the picture. Complete the sentences with the correct possessives.

1. It's my _____ house.
2. It's my _____ car.
3. It's my _____ skateboard.
4. They're my _____ kites.

5 Rewrite the sentences in Exercise 4 in two different ways. Use possessive adjectives and possessive pronouns.

1. It's _____ house. It's _____.
2. It's _____ car. It's _____.
3. It's _____ skateboard. It's _____.
4. They're _____ kites. They're _____.

6 Complete the sentences with *always*, *usually*, *often*, *sometimes*, or *never*. More than one answer may be possible.

Jean	Michelle	Ella
Watches TV every day from 7:00–9:00 p.m.	Watches TV most Mondays from 4:00–6:00 p.m. and watches movies every other weekend	Watches movies once in a while on Sundays

1. Michelle _____ watches TV on Tuesdays.
2. Jean _____ watches TV from 7:00 to 9:00 p.m.
3. Ella _____ watches movies on Sundays.
4. Michelle _____ watches movies on the weekends.

14 | Review 1

7 Rewrite the sentences and questions to make them correct.

1. When types of movies does your parents likes?
   _____

2. Does they likes comedies?
   _____

3. They doesn't call him Mr. Sparrow.
   _____

4. She teach at my school three times a week.
   _____

8 Complete the conversation.

always	so
hate watching	Tell me about it.
horror	That's interesting.
I think	want to watch
need to see	Whose
Really	

Mark: Let's go see *Godzilla* at the theater.

Anna: Maybe. ¹_____

Mark: Well, it's a ²_____ movie about a big monster.

Anna: I dislike those types of movies. I ³_____ a comedy on TV. *Modern Family* is on tonight.

Mark: ⁴_____? You can ⁵_____ watch TV. But the movie is only at the theater this week.

Anna: ⁶_____ we can rent *Godzilla* and watch it at home.

Mark: I ⁷_____ movies on a TV! You ⁸_____ horror movies on a big screen!

Anna: ⁹_____ ¹⁰_____ flat screen TV is it? Don't you have this big TV ¹¹_____ that you can watch movies?

9 Answer the questions about your favorite movies and TV shows. Write complete sentences.

1. What is your favorite movie? What type of movie is it?
   _____
   _____

2. How often do you watch TV?
   _____
   _____

3. What types of movies or TV shows do you dislike? Why do you dislike them?
   _____
   _____
   _____

4. How do you feel about documentaries? Why?
   _____
   _____
   _____

3 Spending Habits

VOCABULARY Places to shop

1 Find 10 more words for places to shop.

> ATM   bank   ✓bookstore   clothing store
> department store   electronics store
> food court   jewelry store   music store
> pharmacy   shoe store   sporting goods store

T	Z	G	V	U	E	W	U	F	P	G	O	C	X	F	H	N	L	J
A	G	E	L	E	C	T	R	O	N	I	C	S	S	T	O	R	E	Q
Q	Z	A	T	M	W	P	D	J	B	P	M	U	N	N	A	E	J	K
N	M	U	S	I	C	S	T	O	R	E	N	D	P	D	A	F	G	R
D	N	N	D	E	P	A	R	T	M	E	N	T	S	T	O	R	E	A
F	Y	V	L	J	E	W	E	L	R	Y	S	T	O	R	E	N	T	P
B	O	O	K	S	T	O	R	E	X	T	B	A	N	K	Y	R	M	V
F	S	P	O	R	T	I	N	G	G	O	O	D	S	S	T	O	R	E
I	S	H	O	E	S	T	O	R	E	C	P	H	A	R	M	A	C	Y
V	N	W	D	M	I	C	L	O	T	H	I	N	G	S	T	O	R	E
Y	I	Q	M	S	Z	D	L	B	F	O	O	D	C	O	U	R	T	P

2 Put the places from Exercise 1 in the correct columns. Use each word only once.

Where to get . . .			
things you can wear	things you can play	things you need to pay for things	many different types of things
shoe store			

things you need to be healthy	things to read	things to eat

3 Where can you do these things? Write places from Exercise 1.

1. My sister bought a new MP3 player at the _electronics store_.

2. I like to read. I want to go to the _____.

3. We can eat lunch at the _____.

4. She saw a pretty necklace at the _____.

5. They went to the _____ to buy a new tennis racket.

6. We can find a wedding gift at the _____. They sell everything.

7. When my little brother is sick, I buy medicine from the _____.

8. I take money out from the _____ to go to my favorite stores.

4 Complete the sentences with your own information.

1. My favorite type of store is _a clothing store. I like to buy jeans._

2. I always shop at the _____

3. I never shop at the _____

4. On the weekend, I dislike going to the _____

5. I sometimes go to the _____

16 | Unit 3

GRAMMAR Present continuous review

1 Complete the chart using the present continuous.

Affirmative	Negative
1. I _'m getting_ lunch at the café. (get)	I _'m not getting_ lunch at the food court.
2. My friend Hal _____ at the bank now. (wait)	He _____ at the electronics store.
3. My teacher _____ at the clothing store today. (shop)	My teacher _____ at the bookstore.
4. My sister _____ a book bag online for school. (buy)	She _____ a backpack at the department store.
5. The class _____ in their notebooks right now. (write)	They _____ on their laptops.

GRAMMAR Simple present vs. present continuous

2 Complete the questions and answers. Use the present continuous or the simple present.

1. What _are_ you _watching_ right now? (watch)

   I'm watching a movie. I _'m not watching_ TV. (not watch)

2. What _____ she _____ today? (do)

   She's not running in a race. She _____ on Mondays. (study)

3. Where _____ they _____ right now? (go)

   They _____ to the beach. (go) They _____ when it's sunny. (not hike)

4. _____ you _____ about a mall in Dubai today? (write)

   Yes, I am. But I usually _____ about shopping malls. (not write)

5. _____ he _____ clothes now? (change)

   No, he's not. He usually _____ his basketball uniform home. (wear)

3 Complete the conversation with the correct forms of the verbs.

| ✓ are | buy | do | look | study |
| are | ✓do | get | shop | walk |

Alana: Hello, Vivian. What ¹_are_ you ²_doing_?

Vivian: Hi. I ³_____ with my sister, Haley. We ⁴_____ at hats.

Alana: Hats?

Vivian: Well, Haley is. But I'm ⁵_____ a hat. I need to buy sneakers for basketball. ⁶_____ you ⁷_____ your dog outside?

Alana: I wish! I'm ⁸_____ for the science test.

Vivian: Oh, too bad. I hate ⁹_____ homework on the weekend.

Alana: Me, too. But I hate ¹⁰_____ bad grades more.

4 Write sentences about you. Use the present continuous or the simple present.

1. What are you doing right now?

   I'm studying English.

2. Where are you right now?

   _____

3. Do you usually study English at this time?

   _____

4. What are you writing with right now?

   _____

Unit 3 | 17

VOCABULARY Money verbs

1 Circle the seven money verbs.

~~save~~ ~~earn~~ ~~borrow~~ ~~spend~~ ~~lend~~ ~~deposit~~ ~~withdraw~~

2 Match each word with its opposite.

1. borrow — a. spend
2. deposit — b. save
3. earn — c. lend
4. spend — d. withdraw

3 Correct the sentences.

1. When he needs money, he ~~lends~~ *withdraws* it at the ATM.
2. I earn my allowance by putting it in the bank.
3. My cousin deposits money from me.
4. We work after school to withdraw money to buy a bike.
5. I prefer to borrow my money on concerts, not on clothes.

4 Write sentences describing a good friend or someone in your family. Use the money verbs.

1. (save) *My friend Bill saves his money every month.*
2. (earn) _____
3. (deposit) _____
4. (withdraw) _____
5. (spend) _____
6. (borrow) _____
7. (lend) _____

18 | Unit 3

GRAMMAR Quantifiers

1 Circle the correct quantifiers.

1. I don't have **many** / **(any)** money until Friday.
2. Are there **much** / **many** T-shirts on sale?
3. She's not old **enough** / **some** to babysit.
4. How **a lot of** / **much** time do you have to study tonight?
5. Kevin earns **some** / **any** money selling cookies.
6. They don't have **much** / **a lot of** people on their team.

2 Complete the chart with quantifiers. More than one answer may be possible.

With countable plural nouns
1. How ___many___ sweaters do you have?
2. I have _____ sweaters.
3. I don't have _____ sweaters.
4. Are there _____ sweaters in your closet?

With uncountable nouns
5. How ___much___ money do you save every month?
6. I save _____ money every month.
7. I don't save _____ money every month.
8. Is there _____ money for the trip?

3 Complete the conversation with the correct quantifiers.

| any | How many | some |
| enough | ✓How much | |

Jackie: The concert tickets are on sale now. Do you want to buy one?

Andrew: I want to buy two. ¹ ___How much___ is a ticket?

Jackie: They're $25.00 each.

Andrew: Oh no! I don't have ² _____ money. Can I borrow ³ _____ money?

Jackie: Sorry. I don't have ⁴ _____ money either. Who is the other ticket for?

Andrew: It's for Erika.

Erika: Andrew! I'll buy our tickets. ⁵ _____ times do I have to tell you that?!?

4 Complete the questions with quantifiers. Then answer the questions with your own information.

1. How ___many___ tests do you have this week?
   I don't have any tests this week.

2. Are there _____ cafés in your town?
   _____
   _____

3. How _____ time do you spend online every day?
   _____
   _____

4. How _____ students are in your class?
   _____
   _____

5. Do you have _____ time to watch movies on the weekend?
   _____
   _____

6. How _____ times do you text each day?
   _____
   _____

Unit 3 | 19

CONVERSATION Shopping time

1 Put the words in the correct order to make sentences a shopper might say. Then match the sentences to the responses.

1. like / some / to / sneakers / I'd / buy / .

   I'd like to buy some sneakers. **d**

2. Can / on / try / I / them / ?

   _____

3. ones / prefer / red / I'd / those / .

   _____

4. them / I'll / take / !

   _____

a. The red ones are very nice. Here, try them on.

b. Of course. Here you are.

c. OK. That'll be $39.

d. OK. How about these green ones?

2 Put the sentences in order to make a conversation.

__1__ **Brandon:** I'd like to buy <u>some sneakers</u>, please.

____ **Clerk:** OK. That'll be $59.

____ **Brandon:** <u>Good. They're big enough.</u> I'll take them.

____ **Clerk:** OK. How <u>about these blue basketball sneakers</u>?

____ **Brandon:** Hmm. I'd prefer <u>ones to play basketball in</u>.

____ **Clerk:** OK. Try <u>these</u>. How do they fit?

____ **Brandon:** <u>Size 11</u>.

____ **Clerk:** Of course. What size do you wear?

____ **Brandon:** Can I try <u>them</u> on?

____ **Clerk:** OK. How about <u>these black ones? They're great for running</u>.

3 Rewrite the conversation in Exercise 2 in order. Change the underlined words to use your own ideas.

1. **You:** I'd like to buy _____, please.
2. **Clerk:** _____
3. **You:** _____
4. **Clerk:** _____
5. **You:** _____
6. **Clerk:** _____
7. **You:** _____
8. **Clerk:** _____
9. **You:** _____
10. **Clerk:** _____

READING TO WRITE

1 Read the review. Label the information with the words and phrases.

don't like   like   ✓name of product   recommendation   the price   where to buy

Rain Boots

name of product
¹Splashy Rain Boots are for sale ²online. They really keep your feet dry. ³They come in lots of fun colors, like purple. ⁴The price is good, too: only $29. The boots are high enough to step in deep puddles on rainy days. ⁵The only problem is that they are too big. I am usually a size 7, but I got these in size 6. ⁶When you order them, buy one size smaller!

2 Circle the correct answers.

1. My cell phone is great. **(Buy)** / **Don't buy** one like mine.
2. **Get** / **Don't get** these T-shirts today. Wait until Saturday and save $10.
3. The hotel is very pleasant. **Spend** / **don't spend** your next vacation here!
4. The fruit at this store is old. **Shop** / **Don't shop** here if you want fresh fruit!
5. These sweaters come in many colors. **Buy** / **Don't buy** more than one if you can.
6. The concert seats aren't very good. Let's **get** / **not get** the tickets.

3 Write recommendations about products you use. Use imperatives.

1. _Don't buy the newest cell phone._
2. _____
3. _____
4. _____
5. _____

Unit 3 | 21

4 Our Heroes

VOCABULARY Cool jobs

1 Use the pictures to complete the crossword.

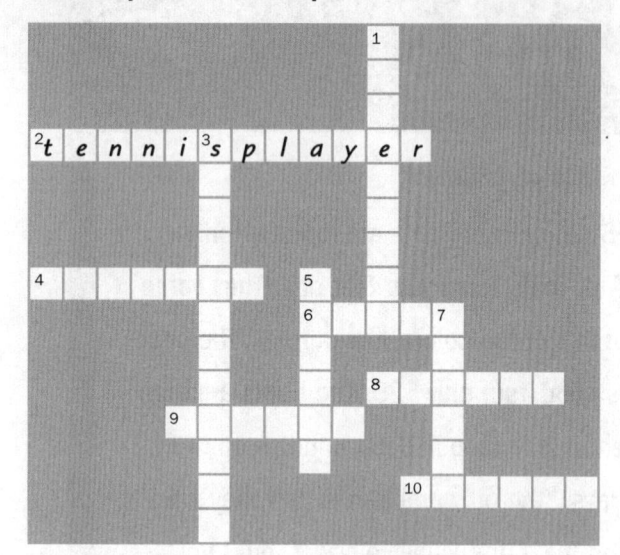

²t e n n i ³s p l a y e r

ACROSS
2.
4.
6.
8.
9.
10.

DOWN
1.
3.
5.
7.

2 Circle the correct answers.

1. Which job is a sports job?
   a. painter   b. writer   c. soccer player

2. Which job is an academic job?
   a. scientist   b. runner   c. singer

3. Which job is a job in the arts?
   a. scientist   b. soccer player   c. writer

4. Which is NOT a job in the arts?
   a. dancer   b. painter   c. runner

3 Write a sentence about a famous person for each of the jobs listed below.

1. scientist _Neil deGrasse Tyson is a famous scientist._
2. tennis player _____
3. soccer player _____
4. actor _____
5. singer _____

4 Complete the sentences with the jobs from Exercise 1.

I think a lot about what type of job I would like. I love sports! I'm a ¹ _soccer player_ on the school team. I'm also a ² _____, but I'm not on the team. I just play my brother. I'm not a very fast ³ _____. I like sports, but I don't think I want to do sports as a job.

I don't want to work in arts or entertainment. I'm not good at making pictures, so I don't want to be a ⁴ _____. I don't have a good voice, so I can't be a ⁵ _____. And I don't like to talk in front of an audience, so I don't want to be an ⁶ _____. I'm athletic, but I don't move well, so I can't be a ⁷ _____.

I like rules, but I don't like to argue, so I wouldn't want to be a ⁸ _____. I'm not very good at math or chemistry, so I wouldn't want to be a ⁹ _____. I do like telling stories and reading books, so maybe I could be a ¹⁰ _____. I could work for a sports magazine!

22 | Unit 4

GRAMMAR Simple past statements review and *ago*

1 Complete the chart with verbs in the simple past.

Affirmative statements	Negative statements
She _____ a millionaire at age 21.	She __*wasn't*__ a millionaire at age 20.
I __*was*__ in a play a month __*ago*__.	I _____ in a movie last month.
He _____ in a restaurant.	He __*didn't work*__ as a lawyer.
They __*tried*__ to play tennis a week __*ago*__.	They _____ to play last month.
She _____ a race in 2010.	She __*didn't run*__ any races in 2014.
We __*won*__ the match a year _____.	We _____ the match.

2 Write the correct forms of the verbs.

1. I __*lived*__ in São Paulo when I was five. (live)
2. His father _____ in Hong Kong five years ago. (work)
3. They _____ for running shoes last weekend. (shop)
4. We _____ surfing when we were at the beach. (try)
5. She _____ a job with the New York City Ballet. (not get)
6. The band _____ their first video in 2011. (not make)
7. I _____ a job as a singer three months ago. (not have)
8. She _____ a popular book in 2007. (not write)

3 Write statements about Daniella using the simple past. Use information from the chart.

	Affirmative	Negative
1. live	Mexico City	Paris
2. want to be	painter	doctor
3. has	friends	brothers or sisters
4. work	in a library	in a café
5. win	awards	medals

1. *Daniella lived in Mexico City. She didn't live in Paris.*
2. _____
3. _____
4. _____
5. _____

4 Complete the sentences with the simple past and your own ideas. Write affirmative or negative statements.

1. I __*was in sixth grade*__ two years ago. (be)
2. I _____ five years ago. (live)
3. My friends and I _____ last year. (like)
4. I _____ last month. (play)
5. My parents _____ for three years before I was born. (be)
6. I _____ when I was five. (want to be)

VOCABULARY Adjectives of personality

1 Put the letters in the correct order to make personality words.

1. MALC _____calm_____
2. DIKN _____
3. NUFYN _____
4. EVBAR _____
5. EITUQ _____
6. ROSESIU _____
7. BRSTNUOB _____
8. LEFUCERH _____
9. DREFYLIN _____

2 Match the definitions with the correct words from Exercise 1. Write the number for each.

____5____ doesn't talk a lot

_____ makes you laugh a lot

_____ doesn't get excited

_____ isn't scared of things

_____ is always happy and smiling

_____ likes to meet new people

_____ studies all the time

_____ won't listen to others

_____ helps others and is nice

3 Complete the paragraph with the personality words from Exercise 1. Then write the name of each girl beside the picture.

| brave | ✓cheerful | funny | kind | serious |

My name is Stella. I want to tell you about my friends. First, there's Emily. She is very ¹ _cheerful_ . If you want to have a party, she will make it fun. My friend Tina is very ² _____. She makes me laugh. My friend Mala is the ³ _____ one. She's not scared of anything. Jane is my nicest friend. She is very ⁴ _____. Then there's Anna. She studies a lot, so my friends say that she's ⁵ _____.

_____

_____

_____Emily_____

_____

_____

4 Use the adjectives of personality to write sentences about yourself, your friends, and your family.

1. _My brother is funny._
2. _____
3. _____
4. _____
5. _____

GRAMMAR Simple past questions review and *ago*

1 Match the questions with the correct answers.

1. How was she few minutes ago?
2. Where was she?
3. Did you see the shark?
4. How long ago did it start following her?
5. Who did you call?
6. What did they say?
7. Was she scared then?

a. It started five minutes ago.
b. Yes, I did.
c. I called the beach patrol.
d. She was happy and having fun.
e. She was far from the beach.
f. Yes, she was!
g. They said to wave at her and point to the shark.

2 Complete the questions.

1. What ___*did*___ you ___*do*___ yesterday? (do)
   We went camping.
2. _____ you _____ the fire? (see)
   Yes, we did.
3. Where _____ you when it started? (be)
   We were in the tent.
4. How long ago _____ it _____? (start)
   It started two hours ago.
5. Where _____ you _____? (run)
   We ran up that hill.
6. Where _____ they _____ the campers? (put)
   They put them on the fire truck.

3 Write questions in the simple past.

1. how / he / a few hours / ago
   How was he a few hours ago?
2. it / start / a few minutes / ago
3. what / they / talk about
4. he / study / last night
5. they / at the library
6. why / you / think / that
7. we / sad / last year

4 Answer these questions with your own information.

1. How did you feel a few minutes ago?
   I was calm a few minutes ago.
2. Did you study English last night?
3. Where did you go last week?
4. Who did you text yesterday?
5. Did you see a movie last weekend?

CONVERSATION Everyday heroes

1 Put the words in the correct order to make sentences to complete the conversation.

1. **A:** Who's / hero / your / ?
   Who's your hero?

2. **B:** think / I / are / athletes / heroes / .
   _____

3. **A:** mean / you / do / What / ?
   _____

4. **B:** mean / athletes / I / hard / train / .
   _____
   at / are / the / They / their / best / sport / .
   _____

5. **A:** that / winners / heroes / Are / you / are / saying / ?
   _____
   _____

6. **B:** Not exactly. / make / that / What / to / say / heroes / is / us / try / I'm / harder / trying / .
   _____
   _____

2 Circle the phrases in Exercise 1 that ask for and give clarification.

3 Use the phrases to complete the conversations. There is more than one way to complete them.

> Are you saying that
> I mean
> ✓ What do you mean?
> What I'm trying to say is that

1. **A:** My heroes have always been cowboys.
   B: _What do you mean?_

2. **A:** I don't think business people are heroes.
   B: _____ they can't be heroes?

3. **A:** _____ superheroes are like real people.
   B: Oh, I see.

4. **A:** You think celebrities don't want to help others?
   B: _____ celebrities want to be _famous_ for helping others.

READING TO WRITE

1 Read about a hero. Then fill out the chart about her.

My hero is Serena Williams. She is famous (because) she is a great tennis player. In 2002, she became number one in the world for the first time. From 2002 to 2003, she held all four Grand Slam titles at the same time. She also won four Olympic medals.

I admire Serena Williams because she is a great tennis player. I also admire her because she is very strong and can come back to win after almost losing. Since she was brave enough to overcome her injuries, she can still play. She's also very kind and built a school in Kenya, Africa. Due to these reasons, she's my hero.

Who	Serena Williams
Her job	_____
Her personality	_____, _____, _____
Heroic things she has done	_____
Why I admire her	_____

2 Circle the connector words (*because, due to, since*) in Exercise 1. Then rewrite the sentences using different connector words.

1. *Since she is a great tennis player, she is famous.*
2. _____
3. _____
4. _____
5. _____

3 Choose the correct connector words.

1. I admire Jane Goodall **since** / **(due to)** her work with chimpanzees.
2. Rick helps ocean animals **due to** / **because** he used to train them.
3. Erika has raced motorcycles **because** / **since** 2011.
4. **Due to** / **Since** his last movie, he's no longer popular.
5. **Since** / **Because** she works very hard, she is my role model.

4 Write sentences about your role model. Use connector words.

   because   due to   since

1. *The Dalai Lama is my role model because he is so calm.*
2. _____
3. _____
4. _____
5. _____

Unit 4 | 27

REVIEW UNITS 3–4

1 Match the descriptions with the correct pictures. Then write the names of the places.

1. a place to buy shoes ____ _____
2. a place to get something to eat ____ _____
3. a place to deposit money ____ _____
4. a place to get medicine ____ _____
5. a place to buy many different things ____ _____

a. 
b. 
c. 
d. 
e.

2 Look at the pictures. Circle the correct answers.

Jeff: Since I like to study wildlife, I want to be a ¹**lawyer / runner / scientist**. Because I'm ²**brave / funny / cheerful**, I can work with dangerous animals like snakes. And I'm ³**quiet / stubborn / serious**, so I can get close to them.

Nina: I love music. Ever since I was little, I've wanted to be a ⁴**singer / actor / painter**. I'm a good performer because I can be ⁵**kind / calm / stubborn** on stage. But I also need to be ⁶**quiet / serious / friendly** so I can talk to the audience between songs.

Alex: I love reading stories. Some people say I'm ⁷**cheerful / funny / kind** because I tell jokes. Other people say I'm ⁸**cheerful / serious / friendly** because I read a lot. I think I'd like to be a ⁹**soccer player / dancer / writer**. Then I could write funny stories.

3 Complete the sentences with the present continuous or simple present forms of the verbs.

1. I _____ (not watch) a movie right now.
2. She _____ (earn) money at her weekend job.
3. We usually _____ (spend) money on video games.
4. They _____ (deposit) the money into my account right now.
5. She _____ (lend) her cousins money every month.

4 Circle the correct answers.

1. A: How _____ money do you have?
   a. many   b. much   c. enough
   B: I have _____ money.
   a. any   b. enough   c. don't

2. A: Are there _____ shoes in your closet?
   a. many   b. how much   c. much
   B: Yes, _____.
   a. there is   b. there are   c. there aren't
   B: No, _____.
   a. there is   b. there isn't   c. there aren't

3. A: How _____ books do you have?
   a. much   b. any   c. many
   B: I don't have _____ books.
   a. many   b. much   c. some

4. A: _____ did you ride your bike last weekend?
   a. Where   b. When   c. Why
   B: I _____ to the beach.
   a. biking   b. am going   c. biked to bike

5. **A:** Where is Tim _____ on his vacation?
   a. go   b. going to go   c. went

   B: He _____ to the mountains.
   a. 's going   b. are going   c. goes to go

5 Circle the correct words. Then match the questions with the correct answers.

1. When **was / were / did** she go to China? _____
2. **Was / Were / Did** Lara play soccer last summer? _____
3. **Was / Were / Did** your friends visit last night? _____
4. Where **was / were / did** your cousins last weekend? _____
5. Where **was / were / did** Jason study last night? _____

a. No, she didn't.
b. They were at the pool.
c. She went in June.
d. He studied at the library.
e. Yes, they did.

6 Complete the sentences with the simple past.

Arline	Seth	Kyla
– study English on Wednesday	– play soccer Monday	– act in a movie in April
– go to Canada in June	– join soccer team in February	

1. Seth _____ soccer on Monday.
2. Arline _____ English on Wednesday.
3. Kyla _____ in a movie in April.
4. Arline _____ to Canada in June.
5. Seth _____ a soccer team in February.

7 Complete the conversations.

a lot of	lend
Are you saying that	much
borrow	started
enough	

Arthur: I really want to buy this hoodie!

Brittany: What do you like about it?

Arthur: It's made by a company that Bono ¹_____ in 2005. He's my hero.

Brittany: ²_____ you'd buy that just because of Bono?

Arthur: Well, it looks cool, too.

Clerk: May I help you?

Arthur: I'd like to buy this hoodie.

Clerk: Here you are. That'll be $79.

Brittany: That's ³_____ money!

Arthur: Oh no! I don't have ⁴_____ money! Can I ⁵_____ some?

Brittany: I don't have that ⁶_____ money either. Maybe your hero Bono can ⁷_____ it to you!

8 Answer the questions about your hero or role model. Write complete sentences.

1. Who is your hero or role model?
   _____
2. What is his or her job?
   _____
3. What heroic things does he or she do?
   _____
4. What is his or her personality like?
   _____
5. Why do you admire him or her?
   _____
6. When were you brave or heroic?
   _____

5 It's a Mystery!

VOCABULARY Action verbs

1 Label the pictures with the words.

caught	fell	ran
chased	hid	stole
✓climbed	jumped	threw

1. _climbed_
2. _____ 
3. _____ 
4. _____ 
5. _____ 
6. _____ 
7. _____ 
8. _____ 
9. _____ 

2 Complete the story. Use the action verbs from Exercise 1.

The squirrel saw a nut up high in the tree. He ¹ _climbed_ the tree. The squirrel got the nut, but then a bird flew by, and the squirrel ² _____ out of the tree. But the squirrel still had the nut!

But the bird wanted the nut. The bird ³ _____ the squirrel. The squirrel ⁴ _____ behind the tree. He ⁵ _____ the nut under a leaf. Then the bird ⁶ _____ the nut.

As the bird flew away, the squirrel ⁷ _____ up on a log. He ⁸ _____ the bird by the leg.

But the bird ⁹ _____ the nut into the pond. The squirrel let go of the bird's leg. This time, no one got the nut!

3 Correct the sentences. Use the simple past.

1. I ~~climb~~ _climbed_ trees a lot when I was young.
2. She said she never steal anything.
3. They hides the key under a rock.
4. She throw the ball really fast.
5. I catched the ball in my glove.
6. Did you see where she run?
7. The apple fells off the tree.
8. They jumpeds over the hole.
9. The dog chase his tail for an hour.

4 Write sentences using the action verbs from Exercise 1. Think of sports you play or activities you do. Use your own information.

1. _I climbed a tree last weekend._
2. _____
3. _____
4. _____
5. _____

GRAMMAR Past continuous; adverbs of time

1 Match the questions with the answers.

1. What were you doing?
2. What was your friend Kevin doing?
3. What was the thief doing?
4. Was the police officer chasing her?
5. What was the thief wearing?
6. Was Kevin taking a picture with his phone?

a. He was using his phone.
b. Yes, he was.
c. No! He was texting and didn't see it.
d. I was buying a hat.
e. She was wearing a baseball cap.
f. She was stealing a hoodie.

2 Read the blog entry. Then answer the questions. Use the past continuous.

My Exciting Day
by Ken

Yesterday was an interesting day. I was skateboarding to school at 8:00 a.m. At about 8:05 a.m., I was passing the bank, and a man ran by me. He was carrying a bag, but he didn't look like he was exercising. He wasn't wearing running shoes. Next, a police officer ran up to me and asked if he could use my skateboard. I let him, of course. Then the police officer was skateboarding down the street! He was chasing the man with the bag. The police officer skated in front of the thief, and the thief fell. The police officer caught him!

1. What was Ken doing at 8:00 a.m.?
   He was skateboarding to school at 8:00 a.m.
2. What did Ken notice about the man's shoes?
   _____
3. What was the man carrying?
   _____
4. How was the police officer chasing the thief?
   _____

3 Unscramble the questions. Then answer the questions with information from the chart.

Last weekend	Last night	At 10:00 p.m.	This morning	At 9:00 a.m.
climbing a mountain	playing video games	sleeping	running a race	chasing a thief

1. night / doing / What / last / she / was / ?
   What was she doing last night?
   She was playing video games.

2. last / she / What / doing / weekend / was / ?
   _____
   _____

3. this / What / she / was / morning / doing / ?
   _____
   _____

4. she / homework / doing / 9:00 a.m. / at / Was / ?
   _____
   _____

5. 10:00 p.m. / at / doing / she / was / What / ?
   _____
   _____

4 Write questions in the past continuous. Answer the questions with your own information.

1. Where / you / live / last year?
   Where were you living last year?
   I was living in Brazil.

2. What / your friend / do / last weekend?
   _____
   _____

3. What / you / wear / yesterday afternoon?
   _____
   _____

4. What / you / do / this morning / at 8:00 a.m.?
   _____
   _____

5. What / you / watch / last night?
   _____
   _____

VOCABULARY Adverbs of manner

1 Find eight more adverbs of manner.

| ✓badly | happily | loudly | quietly | terribly |
| carefully | hard | quickly | slowly | well |

W	E	H	A	P	P	I	L	Y
E	Q	U	I	E	T	L	Y	A
L	H	A	R	D	W	E	L	L
L	T	E	R	R	I	B	L	Y
Q	U	I	C	K	L	Y	A	R
C	A	R	E	F	U	L	L	Y
E	L	O	U	D	L	Y	Y	I
E	E	A	S	L	O	W	L	Y
E	K	E	B	A	D	L	Y	R

2 Match each word with its opposite.

1. sadly — a. slowly
2. loudly — b. happily
3. well — c. badly
4. quickly — d. quietly

3 Complete the paragraph with the correct words.

| carefully | ✓ happily | hard | quickly | terribly |

I was ¹ _happily_ playing my video game last night. It was a difficult game. I didn't want to make any mistakes, so I was playing ² _____. I was trying really ³ _____, and maybe that's why I didn't hear the noise at first. But then it got louder. And then there was a bright light outside the window. I paused the game and went to the window. As I opened the curtain to look, an orange light ⁴ _____ flew by. And then it was gone. I don't know what it was! I was a little scared. After that, I went back to my game, and I played ⁵ _____.

4 Correct the incorrect sentences. Write *correct* if no changes are needed.

1. They did badly on the test. __correct__
2. He played the piano ~~terrible~~. __terribly__
3. The thief ran quickly. _____
4. I tried hardly to win the tennis match. _____
5. The turtle was walking slow. _____
6. We happily sang the birthday song. _____
7. The truck drove by loud. _____
8. We spoke quiet during the movie. _____
9. She was making the model careful. _____

5 Use adverbs of manner to answer the questions with your own information.

1. How do you read?
   I read slowly so I can enjoy the story.

2. How do you spend your money?
   _____

3. Do you walk slowly or quickly?
   _____

4. Do you play tennis well or badly?
   _____

GRAMMAR Simple past vs. past continuous; *when* and *while*

1 Underline the past continuous.

While my sister and I <u>were watching</u> a movie, our dog came into the living room with us. When we were watching the exciting part, the dog started barking. My sister didn't notice the noise. But I did. So I put the dog out in the yard when my sister wasn't looking. Then I was getting snacks for us while my sister watched the movie. The phone was ringing while I was in the kitchen. I told my sister to answer it. She didn't, so I did. It was our neighbor. He saw our dog two blocks away! I gave my sister the snacks. Then I went out to look for the dog. She was watching another movie when I came home with the dog.

2 Match the phrases to make sentences.

1. I was playing soccer well
2. Helen saw the thief grab a hat
3. I heard the fire alarm
4. When we were hiking,
5. While it was raining,

a. while I was cooking dinner.
b. we stayed dry inside.
c. when I scored a goal.
d. we saw a deer with its baby.
e. while we were shopping.

3 Complete the sentences with *when* or *while*. Sometimes both answers are possible.

1. The picture fell loudly ___when / while___ my brothers were playing.
2. I was using the computer _____ I heard the news.
3. _____ the team won, he was cheering loudly.
4. _____ she was surfing, she saw a shark.
5. I was hiking _____ I heard someone singing.
6. _____ he was playing the piano, we were listening happily.

4 Complete the conversation with the simple past or past continuous forms of the verbs.

Mark: Hey, I called you last night at 9:00.

Steve: I know. Sorry. I was watching the game when you ¹___called___ (call).

Mark: Yeah, well, while I ²_____ (watch) the game, our TV broke!

Steve: No! You missed the game! What ³_____ (happen) when it broke?

Mark: Spain was playing well when their center ⁴_____ (fall). The TV broke after that.

Steve: Well, you didn't miss much. After that, Spain was losing badly. I ⁵_____ (turn) the TV off when the game was almost over.

Mark: You didn't watch the ending! Do you know who won?

Steve: Yeah, I ⁶_____ (see) the headline when I was checking my email. Spain lost.

5 Use the verbs to write five sentences about events that were interrupted. Use your own information or write about someone you know.

| cooking | reading | ✓sleeping |
| playing | running | walking |

1. *I was sleeping when the storm began.*
2. _____
3. _____
4. _____
5. _____

CONVERSATION An unusual dream

1 Complete the conversation. Put the words in the correct order to make sentences. More than one answer may be possible.

1. **Mei:** I / you / the / about / Did / movie / tell / ?

   Did I tell you about the movie? The one about a guy named Jeff who has these weird neighbors?

2. **Carlos:** No. / me / Tell / it / about / .

   _____

3. **Mei:** Jeff / the / was / sleeping / beginning, / In / .

   _____

4. Then / while / looked / talking / on / the / out of / the / was / window / Jeff / phone / he / .

   _____
   _____

5. his / watching / neighbors / was / He / .

   _____

6. **Carlos:** they / were / What / doing / ?

   _____

7. **Mei:** was / while / man / A / woman / in / her / bedroom / a letter / hid / reading / a / .

   _____
   _____

8. went / bedroom / there / man / the / the / and / was / screaming / into / Then / .

   _____
   _____

9. **Carlos:** weird / That's / .

   _____

10. happened / what / Then / ?

    _____

2 Choose the correct phrase to tell or react to a story.

Frank: ¹That's weird / (Did I tell you about) the play?

Olga: ²No, what happened? / Then what happened?

Frank: Well, ³**did I tell you / in the beginning**, the actor was saying his lines when the power went out.

Olga: ⁴**In the beginning. / That's weird.**

Frank: Yeah, it was. Then there was a scream in the audience. We thought it was part of the play.

Olga: ⁵**Then what happened? / Did I tell you?**

3 Complete the sentences.

| ✓Did I tell you about | In the beginning |
| That's weird | Then what happened |

Sally: ¹ *Did I tell you about* my ski trip?

Jack: No. What happened?

Sally: ² _____ I was skiing very carefully, and then I got tired. I started skiing badly.

Jack: Oh, oh. ³ _____ ?

Sally: Well, I jumped over a log and I landed badly. I fell into the deep snow. I heard a noise and thought my leg was broken. But my leg was fine.

Jack: ⁴ _____ .

Sally: Yeah, it was strange. I really thought I broke my leg. But it was the sound of my ski breaking!

Jack: That's funny.

READING TO WRITE

1 **Put the parts of the story in order.**

____ But when I got there, the door was locked.
I didn't have a key. At first, I was surprised because I didn't lock the door. So who did?

____ Then I heard barking. My dog was inside.
A few minutes later, he came to the door. Then he jumped on the door.

__1__ It was a dark and stormy night. I was feeding the animals in the barn when I heard the rain.
I closed the barn and ran to the house.

____ In the end, I climbed in through a window.

____ Then I thought maybe his foot locked the door on accident. After that, I was less scared. But I was wet from all the rain!

____ Next, I was scared. What if someone was in the house?

2 **Look at Exercise 1. Draw a square around the beginning and draw an X through the end. Then circle the sequencing words.**

3 **Rewrite the story above. Try to use only one sentence for each part.**

| At first | Later | ✓One night |
| Finally | Next | Then |

1. *One night, it started to rain.*
2. _____ I was surprised that _____.
3. _____ I was afraid that _____.
4. _____ my dog _____.
5. _____ I was less _____.
6. _____ I _____.

Carpets of DAGESTAN

Unit 1 Video 1.1

BEFORE YOU WATCH

1 Look at the pictures from the video. Complete the sentences with the correct words.

| business | carpets | colors | wool |

It takes months to make these beautiful _____. These men work for a carpet _____ in Russia. They buy the _____ from sheep farmers and dye it different _____.

WHILE YOU WATCH

2 Watch the video. Are the sentences true (*T*) or false (*F*)? Correct the false sentences.

1. Dagestan is in southern Russia. _____
2. Khan has a car business. _____
3. He buys wool from his wife's sister. _____
4. Khan's business makes 250 carpets a year. _____
5. It takes four months to make a carpet. _____

3 Watch the video again. Circle the words you hear.

1. People here speak over **30 / 40** languages.
2. He gives work to many **villages / villagers.**
3. The water can't be too hot or too **cool / cold**.
4. Only **men / women** make Khan's carpets.
5. In the evening, many women work on their **homes / farms**.

AFTER YOU WATCH

4 Work with a partner. Take turns saying what you have in your backpack. Where do the items come from?

> I have a water bottle. It comes from China.

A Very INDIAN WEDDING

Unit 1 Video 1.3

BEFORE YOU WATCH

1 Look at the pictures from the video and read the sentences. Match the words with the definitions.

Traditional Indian weddings are often big and beautiful.

Women paint the bride's hands with henna before the wedding.

The bride gives the groom rice during the wedding.

1. wedding _____
2. bride _____
3. henna _____
4. groom _____

a. a woman who is going to be married
b. a special paint
c. a marriage ceremony
d. a man who is going to be married

WHILE YOU WATCH

2 Watch the video. Number the sentences 1–5 in the order you see them.

1. The groom rides a white horse. _____
2. The bride's family dances for her. _____
3. Fifty people work on the flowers. _____
4. The women draw henna on the bride's hands. _____
5. The bride gives the groom rice. _____

3 Watch the video again. Check (✓) the sentences you hear.

1. ❑ Some traditions are hundreds of years old.
2. ❑ People say red henna is a good sign.
3. ❑ They all prepare for the big day.
4. ❑ The groom is waiting.
5. ❑ They walk together today and for life.

AFTER YOU WATCH

4 Work with a partner. Make a list of wedding traditions in your country.

1. bride: white dress
2. groom: dark suit
3. wedding rings
4. music
5. flowers

Unit 1 | 73

A Life on BROADWAY

Unit 2 Video 2.1

BEFORE YOU WATCH

1 Look at the pictures from the video. Do you think the sentences are true (*T*) or false (*F*)?

1. In a musical, the actors sing and dance. _____
2. In most musicals, dogs sing. _____
3. There are many different kinds of jobs in the theater. _____

WHILE YOU WATCH

2 Watch the video. Circle the correct answers.

1. The star of the play is _____ years old.
   a. 10　　　　　　　b. 11　　　　　　　c. 12
2. The director tells the actresses _____ to move.
   a. where　　　　　 b. who　　　　　　c. what
3. The set designer creates the _____.
   a. play　　　　　　b. lights　　　　　c. place
4. People prepare for _____ to put on a play.
   a. weeks　　　　　 b. months　　　　　c. years

3 Watch the video again. Match the adjectives with the nouns you hear.

1. theater _____
2. popular _____
3. lighting _____
4. special _____

a. effects
b. designer
c. musical
d. capital

AFTER YOU WATCH

4 Work with a small group. Complete the chart below. Then discuss: What are some of your favorite plays or movies? Who were the actors? What parts did they play?

Movie / Play	Actor	Part	Actor	Part
X-Men	Hugh Jackman	Wolverine	Jennifer Lawrence	Mystique

> I really liked the new *X-Men* movie. Hugh Jackman was in it. He played Wolverine. Jennifer Lawrence played Mystique.

74 | Unit 2

MUMBAI: *From* COMPUTERS *to* FILM

Unit 2 Video 2.3

BEFORE YOU WATCH

1 Look at the pictures from the video. Circle the correct answers.

   1. These people work **on farms / in offices** in Mumbai, India.

   2. People make thousands of **films / computers** in Mumbai.

WHILE YOU WATCH

2 Watch the video. Number the places and things 1–5 in the order you see them.

   1. a festival _____
   2. a bus _____
   3. a park _____
   4. Mumbai at night _____
   5. a train _____

3 Watch the video again. Are the sentences true (*T*) or false (*F*)? Correct the false sentences.

   1. Mumbai is a rich city. _____
   2. Ten years ago, the population of Mumbai was 20 million. _____
   3. Many people work in modern offices. _____
   4. Traditions are not important here. _____
   5. Some traditional festivals are part of India's film industry. _____

AFTER YOU WATCH

4 Work with a partner. Discuss: What TV shows or movies take place in a big city? What do you learn about the city?

> *Spiderman* takes place in New York City. There are a lot of really big buildings . . . and a lot of people and cars.

Unit 2 | 75

Unusual FUN

BEFORE YOU WATCH

Unit 3 Video 3.1

1. Look at the picture from the video. Check (✔) the sentences you think are probably true.

Mall of the Emirates

1. ❏ The mall has over 1,000 shops.
2. ❏ There are about 50 cinemas here.
3. ❏ You can ride bikes through the mall.
4. ❏ You can go skiing here.

WHILE YOU WATCH

2. Watch the video. What are people doing in the mall? Write short answers to the questions.

   1. Are some people ice skating?   _No, they aren't._
   2. Are some people snowboarding?   _____
   3. Is a little girl holding a balloon? _____
   4. Are the boys looking at skis in the store? _____
   5. Do the boys buy sunglasses?   _____

3. Watch the video again. Circle the correct answers.

   1. Dubai is in the United Arab **States** / **Emirates**.
   2. It's often about **40** / **45** degrees Celsius here.
   3. The mall has **120** / **125** restaurants.
   4. The mall is in the middle of the **Arabian** / **Sahara** Desert.
   5. A lot of kids come here to **eat** / **have fun** with their friends.

AFTER YOU WATCH

4. Work in small groups. Discuss the question at the end of the video: Is there a mall near you? What fun things can you do there? Where do you like to shop?

   > Yes, there is. I like going to movies there . . . and I like visiting the electronics store.

ZERO: PAST and PRESENT

Unit 3 Video 3.3

BEFORE YOU WATCH

1 Look at the pictures from the video. Complete the sentences with the correct numbers.

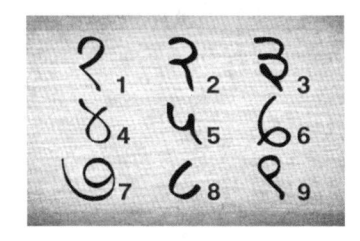

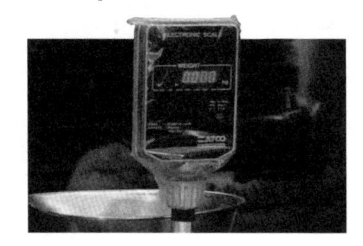

    0   2   10

1. We use the ancient Indian system of _____ digits: 0–9.

2. The number _____ represents nothing, or no quantity.

3. In ancient India, people used the same word for *arms* and for the number _____.

WHILE YOU WATCH

2 Watch the video. Check (✔) the sentences you hear.

1. ❏ From nothing – or zero – came everything.

2. ❏ These ancients used numbers, not words, for quantities.

3. ❏ So, around 11 B.C.E., they invented symbols.

4. ❏ We use numbers with zero and nine.

5. ❏ Think about zero the next time you go shopping.

3 Watch the video again. Complete the sentences with the correct words.

1. The word *digit* comes from the Latin word for _____.

2. We have _____ numbers in our system.

3. Can you imagine life without _____?

4. In computing, there are _____ digits.

5. Prices usually contain _____.

AFTER YOU WATCH

4 Work with a partner. Complete the chart with your information. Then read it to your partner, who will write the information using words, not numbers.

Time	I slept for _____ hours and _____ minutes last night.	
Weight	My backpack weighs about _____ kilos.	
Price	A new laptop costs about _____ pesos.	
Speed	An airplane flies at about _____ kilometers an hour.	

Wildlife HERO

Unit 4 Video 4.1

BEFORE YOU WATCH

1 Look at the pictures from the video. Complete the sentences with the correct words.

| in danger | rhino | wildlife | vet |

1. Animals that live in nature are called _____.

3. A _____ is a large animal with thick skin.

2. A _____ is a doctor who takes care of animals.

4. Some animals are not safe. There are only a few of them in the world. They are _____.

WHILE YOU WATCH

2 Watch the video. Number the animals 1–5 in the order you see them.

1. A giraffe in a truck   _____
2. Two zebras drinking water   _____
3. A rhino running in a field   _____
4. A lion opening its mouth   _____
5. Two elephants playing   _____

3 Watch the video again. Match the phrases to make true sentences.

1. Yanna wants the animals to _____
2. Yanna's job is dangerous because _____
3. Yanna is going to _____
4. At first, the sedative _____
5. Yanna does this job because _____

a. the black rhino is in danger.
b. take the rhino to a new home.
c. the animals are wild.
d. be safe from hunters.
e. makes the rhino fall asleep.

AFTER YOU WATCH

4 Work in a small group. Discuss: Have you, or has someone you know, ever saved an animal? What happened?

> My brother and I once found a kitten. We took it home. We gave it food and water.

The Chilean MINE RESCUE

Unit 4 Video 4.3

BEFORE YOU WATCH

1 Look at the picture from the video. Match the words from the video with the definitions.

1. drill _____
2. miner _____
3. refuge _____
4. rescue _____

a. to save someone from danger
b. a safe place
c. a machine that makes holes
d. a person who works in a mine, deep underground

WHILE YOU WATCH

2 Watch the video. Are the sentences true (*T*) or false (*F*)? Correct the false sentences.

1. In 2010, there was a terrible accident in Chile. _____
2. There were 32 men in the mine. _____
3. The rescue workers found the miners seven days after the accident. _____
4. The miners wrote a note to the rescuers. _____

3 Watch the video again. Circle the correct answers.

1. What happened when the giant rock fell?
   a. It killed many miners.   b. It closed the exit to the mine.   c. It made a deep hole.
2. The rescuers gave the miners a _____.
   a. drill   b. TV   c. phone
3. The men were in the mine for more than _____ months.
   a. two   b. three   c. four
4. How many people watched the final rescue of the miners?
   a. two billion   b. one million   c. one billion

AFTER YOU WATCH

4 Work with a partner. Discuss: Imagine you are trapped inside a mine. What do you feel? Say? How do you keep calm?

> I feel afraid. I'm really worried. I tell my friends that people will save us. I try to breathe deeply.

Mysteries in the MOUNTAINS

Unit 5 Video 5.1

BEFORE YOU WATCH

1 Look at the picture from the video and read the story. Then match the words and the definitions.

Archaeologists study ancient civilizations. They ask questions: Who were these people? How did they live? Some archaeologists were working in Bolivia when they found bones. They looked at the bones with a microscope. They were the bones of a young woman . . .

1. archaeologist _____
2. civilization _____
3. bones _____
4. microscope _____

a. the hard, white pieces that form the frame of a human or animal body
b. a tool that makes small things look bigger
c. a scientist who studies ancient cultures
d. a culture; a society

WHILE YOU WATCH

2 Watch the video. Are the sentences (*T*) or false (*F*)? Correct the false sentences.

1. Last year, Scotty went to Tiwanaku.   _____
2. He was studying an ancient culture.   _____
3. The archaeologists found bones and hair.   _____
4. They found corn next to the bones.   _____
5. The Tiwanaku people grew lots of corn.   _____

3 Watch the video again. Circle the words you hear.

1. They look for clues and **answer / answers** to questions.
2. They lived here in the mountains about **a thousand / two thousand** years ago.
3. The bones were strong and the teeth were **heavy / healthy**.
4. He wanted to look at it **closely / carefully** under a microscope.
5. So, this woman wasn't **from / of** here!

AFTER YOU WATCH

4 Work in a small group. Discuss: Do you like reading about mysteries or watching mysteries on TV? What are some of your favorites?

I like Paper Towns by John Green . . . and Buzz Kill was a great book. I always watch Pretty Little Liars – it's amazing!

The Case of the MISSING WOMAN

BEFORE YOU WATCH   Unit 5 Video 5.3

1 Use the clues and the words to complete the crossword puzzle.

   disappear   interview   missing   remember   search   worry

ACROSS

2. not there, absent

3. to look for

5. to think of someone or something from the past

6. to feel nervous or anxious

DOWN

1. to leave; to go out of sight

4. to ask someone questions, get information

WHILE YOU WATCH

2 Watch the video. Number the sentences 1–5 in the order you see them.

1. The police found Amber's car. _____

2. A video camera showed Amber in a shop. _____

3. The police interviewed Amber's family and friends. _____

4. The police found a woman in a park. _____

5. Amber's car keys were missing. _____

3 Watch the video again. Match the sequencing words you hear with the events.

1. One day, _____   a. Amber was safe.

2. Soon _____   b. police found a woman in a park.

3. Two days ago, _____   c. Amber disappeared from her hometown.

4. Then _____   d. the police found the next clue.

5. Finally, _____   e. Amber was inside the shop alone.

AFTER YOU WATCH

4 Work with a partner. Think of a mystery (a book, a TV show, or a movie) you both know. Take turns describing what happened.

A: In *Veronica Mars*, Veronica has an interview in New York City.
B: Then her boyfriend calls her.
A: Right. So she returns to Neptune . . .

This page intentionally left blank.

Irregular verbs

Base Verb	Simple Past	Past Participle
be	was, were	been
become	became	become
break	broke	broken
bring	brought	brought
build	built	built
buy	bought	bought
catch	caught	caught
choose	chose	chosen
come	came	come
cut	cut	cut
do	did	done
draw	drew	drawn
drink	drank	drunk
drive	drove	driven
eat	ate	eaten
fall	fell	fallen
feel	felt	felt
find	found	found
fit	fit	fit
fly	flew	flown
forget	forgot	forgotten
get	got	gotten
give	gave	given
go	went	gone
grow	grew	grown
hang	hung	hung
have	had	had
hear	heard	heard
hide	hid	hidden
hold	held	held
hurt	hurt	hurt
keep	kept	kept
know	knew	known
leave	left	left

Base Verb	Simple Past	Past Participle
lend	lent	lent
lose	lost	lost
make	made	made
meet	met	met
pay	paid	paid
put	put	put
read	read	read
ride	rode	ridden
ring	rang	rung
run	ran	run
say	said	said
see	saw	seen
sell	sold	sold
send	sent	sent
shut	shut	shut
sing	sang	sung
sit	sat	sat
sleep	slept	slept
speak	spoke	spoken
spend	spent	spent
stand	stood	stood
steal	stole	stolen
swim	swam	swum
take	took	taken
teach	taught	taught
tell	told	told
think	thought	thought
throw	threw	thrown
understand	understood	understood
wear	wore	worn
win	won	won
withdraw	withdrew	withdrawn
write	wrote	written

Answer to Student's Book p. 44 #4 (Who stole the painting?)

The butler and Ray stole the painting. The butler told Clarissa there was a phone call. When she went to answer, he stayed in the garden and then climbed through the living room window. He took the painting and came back out through the window. He passed it to Ray. Ray climbed over the wall and gave it to someone waiting in the street.

Credits

The authors and publishers acknowledge the following sources of copyright material and are grateful for the permissions granted. While every effort has been made, it has not always been possible to identify the sources of all the material used, or to trace all copyright holders. If any omissions are brought to our notice, we will be happy to include the appropriate acknowledgements on reprinting.

p. 2-3 (B/G): Getty Images/Lonely Planet Images; p. 3 (a): Alamy/© Imagebroker/Klaus-Werner Friedrich; p. 3 (b): Alamy/©Radius Images; p. 3 (c): Shutterstock Images/Melis; p. 3 (d): Getty Images/Chicago History Museum; p. 3 (e): Shutterstock Images/Gurgen Bakhshetsyan; p. 3 (f): Alamy/©2d Alan King; p. 3 (g): Getty Images/Retrofile/George Marks; p. 3 (h): Shutterstock Images/Ferenc Szelepcsenyi; p.3 (i): Alamy/©Bon Appetit; p. 3 (j): Shutterstock Images/Subbotina Anna; p. 3 (k): Alamy/©Greg Vaughn; p. 3 (l): Alamy/©Russell Gordon/Danita Delimont; p. 4 (BL): Corbis/Guillermo Granja; p. 4 (BR): Alamy/©Mo Fini; p. 4 (TR): Alamy/©Maria Grazia Casella; p. 5 (BR): Shutterstock Images/Blend Images; p. 6 (TL): Shutterstock Images/Jenoche/A; p. 6 (a): Shutterstock Images/James Steidl; p. 6 (b): Alamy/©Old Paper Studios; p. 6 (c): Shutterstock Images/Nataliya Hora; p. 6 (d): Shutterstock Images/Adrio Communications Ltd; p. 6 (e): Shutterstock Images/Marc Dietrich; p. 6 (f): Alamy/©Yvette Cardozo; p. 6 (g): Getty Images/De Agostini; p. 6 (h): Alamy/©Museum of London; p. 6 (i): Shutterstock Images/Balefire; p. 6 (j): Shutterstock Images/Rob Stark; p. 8 (BR): Shutterstock Images/PhotoNan; p. 8 (CL): Shutterstock Images/Doomu; p. 9 (TR): Getty Images/Adrian Weinbrecht/Digital Vision; p. 10 (B/G): Shutterstock Images/illustrart; p. 10 (TL): Getty Images/Joe Petersburger; p. 10 (TC): Getty Images/GDT; p. 10 (B): Alamy/©Chris Lewington; p. 10 (C): Alamy/©ImageDB; p. 11 (CR): Shutterstock Images/Manczurov; p. 11 (TL): Shutterstock Images/AlexMaster; p. 11 (TR): Shutterstock Images/Zybr78; p. 11 (CL): Shutterstock Images/Mike Flippo; p. 11 (CR): Shutterstock Images/WBB; p. 11 (BR): Alamy/©Urbanmyth; p. 11 (BL): Shutterstock Images/Samuel Borges Photography; p. 12-13 (B/G): Getty Images/John Eder; p. 13 (1): Getty Images/Movie Poster Image Art; p. 13 (2): Alamy/©AF Archive; p. 13 (3): ©DISNEY CHANNEL/THE KOBAL COLLECTION; p. 13 (4): REX/Courtesy Everett Collection; p. 13 (5): REX/Col Pics/Everett; p. 13 (6): Alamy/©Moviestore Collection; p. 13 (7): ©20TH CENTURY FOX/PARAMOUNT/THE KOBAL COLLECTION; p. 13 (8): REX/Courtesy Everett Collection p. 13 (9): Alamy/©AF Archive; p. 14 (T): Shutterstock Images/Bertrand Benoit; p. 14 (B/G): Shutterstock Images/Krivosheev Vitaly; p. 14 (CL): Alamy/©AF Archive; p. 14 (C): THE KOBAL COLLECTION/LUCASFILM/20TH CENTURY FOX; p. 14 (CR): Alamy/©Moviestore Collection Ltd; p. 15 (CR): Getty Images/Adrian Weinbrecht; p. 16 (TL): Shutterstock Images/Szocs Jozsef; p. 16 (1): Getty Images/Jasin Boland/NBC/NBCU Photo Bank; p. 16 (2): Alamy/©Jochen Tack; p. 16 (3): Getty Images/Steve Mort/AFP; p. 16 (4): Alamy/©AF Archive; p. 16 (5): Getty Images/Sonja Flemming/CBS; p. 16 (6): Getty Images/Alexander Tamargo; p. 16 (7): Alamy/©Pictoria Press Ltd; p. 16 (8): Alamy/©Zuma Press; p. 16 (9): Getty Images/Steve Granitz/WireImage; p. 17 (CR): Shutterstock Images/Vovan; p. 18 (TL): Shutterstock Images/Mayakova; p. 18 (BL): Alamy/©Newscast; p. 19 (B/G): Shutterstock Images/Made-in-China; p. 19 (TL): Summit Entertainment/The Kobal Collection; p. 20 (TR): Alamy/©Archives Du 7e Art/Ashutosh Gowariker Productions 12; p. 20 (CR): REX/Everett Collection; p. 20 (BR): ©DHARMA PRODUCTIONS//THE KOBAL COLLECTION; p. 20 (B/G): Shutterstock Images/Loke Yek Mang; p. 20 (TL): Shutterstock Images/Majcot; p. 21 (BR): Shutterstock Images/Kurhan; p. 22-23 (B/G): Getty Images/John Giustina; p. 23 (1): Getty Images/JupiterImages; p. 23 (2): Alamy/©Patti McConville; p. 23 (3): Alamy/©David R.Frazier; p. 23 (4): Alamy/©Alex Segre; p. 23 (5): Alamy/©Patti McConville; p. 23 (6): Alamy/©Lain Masterton; p. 23 (7): Alamy/©P.D.Amedzro; p. 23 (8): Alamy/©Jader Alto; p. 23 (9): Alamy/©Thomas Cockrem; p. 23 (10): Alamy/©Kim Kaminski; p. 23 (11): Shutterstock Images/Racorn; p. 24 (T): Alamy/©Robert Harding Picture Library Ltd; p. 24 (a): Alamy/©Caro; p. 24 (b): Alamy/©D. Hurst; p. 24 (c): Getty Images/Richard I'Anson/Lonely Planet Images; p. 24 (d): Alamy/©Laborant; p. 25 (BR): Corbis/2/Jack Hollingsworth/Ocean; p. 26 (TL): Corbis/Image Source; p. 27 (B): Shutterstock Images/Mark Poprocki; p. 28 (TL): Shutterstock Images/Dmitry Kalinovsky; p. 28 (BL): Shutterstock Images/Elnur; p. 29 (TR): Shutterstock Images/Sashkin; p. 29 (TL): Shutterstock Images/John Kasawa; p. 30 (T): Alamy/©ZUMA Press, Inc; p. 30 (C): Shutterstock Images/Dragi52; p. 30 (TR): Shutterstock Images/Joost Van Uffelen; p. 30 (B/G): Shutterstock Images/Angela Waye; p. 31 (1): Shutterstock Images/Diplomedia; p. 31 (2): Shutterstock Images/Lendy16; p. 31 (3): Alamy/©D. Hurst; p. 31 (4): Shutterstock Images/Studio Smart; p. 31 (5): Shutterstock Images/MTrebbin; p. 31 (6): Shutterstock Images/Julian Rovagnati; p. 32 (C): Corbis/Blue Images; p. 32-33 (B/G): Shutterstock Images/Neirfy; p. 33 (1): Thinkstock/mark wragg/iStock; p. 33 (2): Shutterstock Images/Brocreative; p. 33 (3): Shutterstock Images/Monika Wisniewska; p. 33 (4): Shutterstock Images/yamix; p. 33 (5): Getty Images/Maria Pereira Photograpy/Flickr; p. 33 (6): Corbis/Beau Lark; p. 33 (7): Alamy/©Shotshop GmbH; p. 33 (8): Shutterstock Images/Dmitry Yashkin; p. 33 (9): Alamy/©IE235/Image Source Plus; p. 33 (10): Shutterstock Images/mezzotint; p. 34 (TL): Getty Images/Stephen Dunn; p. 34 (TC): Getty Images/Matthew Lloyd/Bloomberg; p. 34 (TR): REX/Theo Kingma; p. 35 (TR): Alamy/©Photos 12; p. 36 (T): Shutterstock Images/Nils Petersen; p. 36 (a): Alamy/©Jack Hollingsworth/Blend Images; p. 36 (b): Shutterstock Images/Oliveromg; p. 36 (c): Alamy/©KidStock/Blend Images; p. 36 (d): Alamy/©Leah Warkentin/Design Pics Inc; p. 36 (e): Alamy/©Ron Dahlquist/Pacific Stock; p. 36 (f): Shutterstock Images/Piotr Marcinski; p. 36 (g): Alamy/©Kalle Singer/Beyond Fotomedia GmbH; p. 36 (h): Shutterstock Images/Aleksandr Markin; p. 36 (i): Alamy/©Arco Images/De Meester; p. 37 (TR): Shutterstock Images/Shvak; p. 37 (TCR): Shutterstock Images/Rarach; p. 37 (BCR): Getty Images/Image Source; p. 37 (BR): Shutterstock Images/Murengstockphoto; p. 38 (BL): Alamy/©David Grossman; p. 38 (TL): Alamy/©Rosanne Tackaberry; p. 39 (B/G): Getty Images/Jerritt Clark/Stringer; p. 39 (TL): Alamy/©Zuma Press Inc; p. 40 (TL): Getty Images/Pascal Le Segretain; p. 40 (B): Shutterstock Images/Kjersti Joergensen; p. 40 (C): Getty Images/Cameron Spencer; p. 41 (1): Shutterstock Images/Wavebreakmedia; p. 41 (2): Alamy/©PCN Photography; p. 41 (3): Shutterstock Images/Darren Baker; p. 41 (4): Alamy/©[apply pictures]; p. 42-43 (B/G): Getty Images/Marko Stavric Photography; p. 46 (T): Shutterstock Images/Mindscape Studio; p. 46 (1): Alamy/©Agencja Free; p. 46 (2): Alamy/©Blickwinkel; p. 46 (3): Shutterstock Images/Khwi; p. 46 (4): Getty images/Danita Delimont; p. 46 (5): Shutterstock Images/Catalin Petolea; p. 46 (6): Shutterstock Images/Jarry; p. 46 (7): Alamy/©Phovoir; p. 46 (8): Shutterstock Images/Golden Pixels LLC; p. 46 (9): Shutterstock Images/Gow27; p. 47 (T): Corbis/Erik Isakson/Blend Images; p. 48 (BL): Alamy/©MasPix; p. 48 (CL): Alamy/©Blickwinkel; p. 50 (TR): REX/Courtesy Everett Collection; p. 50 (CR): Getty Images/Jeff Neumann/CBS; p. 50 (B/G): Shutterstock Images/Richard Peterson; p. 54-55 (B/G): Corbis/Anna Stowe/LOOP IMAGES; p. 52-52 (B/G): Corbis/Elli Thor Magnusson; p. 56 (TL): Shutterstock Images/guentermanaus; p. 56 (CL): Alamy/©Hemis; p. 56 (TR): Shutterstock Images/Marina Jay; p. 56 (B/G): Shutterstock Images/KayaMe; p. 57 (CL): Alamy/©blickwinkel; p. 58 (TL): Getty Images/Chip Simons; p. 58 (1): Shutterstock Images/Big Pants Production; p. 58 (2): Alamy/©Incamerastock; p. 58 (3): Corbis/Ken Kaminesky/Take 2 Productions; p. 58 (4): Shutterstock Images/Shell114; p. 58 (5): Shutterstock Images/Kamil Macniak; p. 58 (6): Shutterstock Images/Ramona Heim; p. 58 (7): Shutterstock Images/Maxim Ibragimov; p. 58 (8): Shutterstock Images/Sergemi; p. 58 (9): Shutterstock Images/HomeArt; p. 58 (10): Getty Images/J.R.Ball; p. 58 (11):Shutterstock Images/Andrey Armyagov; p. 58 (12): Shutterstock Images/Africa Studio; p. 59 (CR): Shutterstock Images/Jaroslav74; p. 60 (TL): Shutterstock Images/Africa Studio; p. 60 (BL): Shutterstock Images/Gemenacom; p. 61 (TR): Shutterstock Images/Romakoma; p. 62 (T): Shutterstock Images/FCG; p. 62 (TL): Alamy/©Radius Images; p. 62 (CL): Shutterstock Images/EggHeadPhoto; p. 62 (CR): Thinkstock/Stockbyte; p. 62 (BL): Alamy/©Randy Duchaine; p. 62 (B): Shutterstock Images/View Apart; p. 64-65 (B/G): Shutterstock Images/Diversepixel; p. 65 (1): Shutterstock Images/Archiwiz; p. 65 (2): Shutterstock Images/Maksym Dykha; p. 65 (3): Shutterstock Images/AG-PHOTO; p. 65 (4): Shutterstock Images/Alexey Boldin; p. 65 (5): Alamy/©keith morris; p. 65 (6): Shutterstock Images/GeorgeMPhotography; p. 65 (7): Shutterstock Images/Joris van den Heuvel; p. 65 (8): Shutterstock Images/Bloom Design; p. 65 (9): Shutterstock Images/Goldyg; p. 66 (CR): Getty Images/SSPL; p. 66 (T): Shutterstock Images/Sergey Nivens; p. 66 (BR): Shutterstock Images/Joris van den Heuvel; p. 68 (TL): Shutterstock Images/CandyBox Images; p. 68 (a): Shutterstock Images/Showcake; p. 68 (b): Shutterstock Images/Modella; p. 68 (c): Alamy/©Pumkinpie; p. 68 (d): Shutterstock Images/Rob Marmion; p. 68 (e): Alamy/©Mark Sykes; p. 68 (f): Shutterstock Images/Valeri Potapova; p. 68 (g): Alamy/©Maxim Images; p. 69 (CR): Alamy/©Ralph Talmont/Aurora Photos; p. 70 (B): Alamy/©Peter Alvey People; p. 70 (CL): Shutterstock Images/Siberia - Video and Photo; p. 71 (TR): Shutterstock Images/Olga Popova; p. 72 (TL): Shutterstock Images/James Steidl; p. 72 (BR): Alamy/©Ian Dagnall Computing; p. 72 (TR): Shutterstock Images/Fad82; p. 72 (BL): Shutterstock Images/Kitch Bain; p. 72 (B/G): Shutterstock Images/Concept Photo; p. 73 (1): Shutterstock Images/Luis Carlos Torres; p. 73 (2): Shutterstock Images/Maksym Dykha; p. 73 (3): Shutterstock Images/BigKnell; p. 73 (4): Shutterstock Images/Volodymyr Krasyuk; p. 74-75 (B/G): Corbis/Werner Dieterich/Westend61; p. 75 (a): Shutterstock Images/Monkey Business Images; p. 75 (b): Alamy/©Driver's License; p. 75 (c): Alamy/©Cultura Creative; p. 75 (d): Shutterstock Images/Nikola Solev; p. 75 (e): Shutterstock Images/razihusin; p. 75 (f): Shutterstock Images/Joe Gough; p. 75 (g): Shutterstock Images/Karen Grigoryan; p. 75 (h): Alamy/©Ben Molyneux People; p. 75 (i): Corbis/Mark Edward Atkinson/Tracey Lee/Blend Images; p. 75 (j): Shutterstock Images/Monkey Business Images; p. 76 (TL): REX/Bruce Adams;p. 76 (TC): Alamy/©Bill Bachman; p. 77 (BL): Shutterstock Images/MTrebbin; p. 77 (TL): Shutterstock Images/GeniusKp; p. 77 (TR): Shutterstock Images/Arman Zhenikeyev; p. 77 (BR): Shutterstock Images/Irin-k; p. 78 (T): Alamy/©VStock; p. 78 (1): Shutterstock Images/Carsten Reisinger; p. 78 (2): Shutterstock Images/Rob Hyrons; p. 78 (3): Shutterstock Images/Molodec; p. 78 (4): Shutterstock Images/jocic; p. 78 (5): Shutterstock Images/Worker; p. 78 (6): Shutterstock Images/R. Gino Santa Maria; p. 78 (7): Shutterstock Images/Nikkytok; p. 78 (8): Shutterstock Images/Donatas1205; p. 79 (BR): Getty images/Muammer Mujdat Uzel; p. 80 (TL): Shutterstock Images/Bloomua; p. 80 (BL): Alamy/©Denise Hager Catchlight Visual Services; p. 81 (TR): Getty Images/Juanmonino; p. 82 (BL): Alamy/©Steve Skjold; p. 82 (CL): Alamy/©Alaska Stock; p. 82 (B/G): Shutterstock Images/Galyna Andrushko; p. 82 (TL): Alamy/©Gail Mooney-Kelly; p. 82 (T): Shutterstock Images/Galyna Andrushko; p. 83 (1): Shutterstock Images/Roman Samokhin; p. 83 (2): Shutterstock Images/Hal_P; p. 83 (3): Shutterstock Images/EZeePics Studio; p. 83 (4): Alamy/©Mike Kemp; p. 84-85 (B/G): Corbis/Corey Rich/Aurora Open; p .85 (1): Getty Images/Tammy Bryngelson; p. 85 (2): Alamy/©Rob Stark; p. 85 (3): Shutterstock Images/Apples Eyes Studio; p. 85 (4): Alamy/©Nik Taylor; p. 85 (5): Shutterstock Images/Robert Crum; p. 85 (6): Alamy/©Imagebroker; p. 85 (7): Getty Images/Jason Weddington; p. 85 (8): Corbis/Burger/phanie/Phanie Sarl; p. 85 (9): Shutterstock Images/Piotr Marcinski; p. 85 (10): Shutterstock Images/Mahathir Mohd Yasin; p. 86 (CR): Alamy/©Trekandshoot; p. 86 (TR): Shutterstock Images/Dan Thornberg; p. 86 (TL): Shutterstock Images/Ilya Andriyanov; p. 86 (CL): Shutterstock Images/Filatov Alexey; p. 86 (T): Shutterstock Images/Endeavor; p. 87 (CR): Getty Images/Ebby May; p. 88 (T): Shutterstock Images/Varuna; p. 88 (BL): Alamy/©Image Source Plus; p. 88 (BC): Alamy/©Enigma; p. 89 (BR): REX/Andrew Price; p. 90 (TL): Shutterstock Images/Wonderisland; p. 90 (BL): Shutterstock Images/HomeArt; p. 91 (TR): Shutterstock Images/Stefan Pircher; p. 92 (TL): Shutterstock Images/Dr.Morley Read; p. 92 (TC): Shutterstock Images/Kletr; p. 92 (BR): Shutterstock Images/Decha Thapanya; p. 92 (T): Shutterstock Images/Foxy; p. 92 (B/G): Shutterstock Images/Brodtcast; p. 92 (BL): Alamy/©Robert M. Vera; p. 92 (TR): Getty Images/Murray Cooper/Minden Pictures; p. 93 (1,2,3,4): Shutterstock Images/Goa Novi; p. 93 (5,6,7): Shutterstock Images/Flashon Studio; p. 93 (8,9): Shutterstock Images/Iko; p. 94-95 (B/G): Corbis/Tim Pannell; p. 95 (1): Shutterstock Images/Claudia Paulussen; p. 95 (2): Shutterstock Images/Golden Pixels LLC; p. 95 (3): Getty Images/Jupiter Images; p. 95 (4): Shutterstock Images/Christine Langer-Pueschel; p. 95 (5): Shutterstock Images/BlueSkyImage; p. 95 (6): Alamy/©Radius Images; p. 95 (7): Alamy/©Frederic Cirou/PhotoAlto sas; p. 95 (8): Getty Images/Rob Lewine; p. 96 (TL): Alamy/©Zuma Press Inc; p. 96 (TC): Getty Images/Fuse; p. 96 (TR): Alamy/©Gregory James; p. 97 (CL): Alamy/©South West Images Scotland; p. 98 (TL): Getty Images/Mbbirdy; p. 98 (1): Shutterstock Images/PathDoc; p. 98 (2): Shutterstock Images/Guillermo Del Olmo; p. 98 (3): Shutterstock Images/Patrick Foto; p. 98 (4): Shutterstock Images/PathDoc; p. 98 (5): Shutterstock Images/Arvydas Kniuksta; p. 98 (6): Shutterstock Images/Sabphoto; p. 98 (7): Shutterstock Images/Sashahaltam; p. 98 (8): Shutterstock Images/Tracy Whiteside; p. 98 (9): Shutterstock Images/Elena Elisseeva; p. 98 (10): Shutterstock Images/Jeka; p. 100 (TL): Getty Images/Nancy R.Cohen; p. 100 (BL): Getty Images/SW Productions/Photodisc; p. 101 (TR): Alamy/©View Pictures Ltd; p. 102 (B): Shutterstock Images/Roman Sigaev; p. 102 (TR): Shutterstock Images/Focuslight; p. 103 (1): Shutterstock Images/Denise Kappa; p. 103 (2): Shutterstock Images/Studio Vin; p. 103 (3): Alamy/©Niehoff/Imagebroker; p. 103 (4): Shutterstock Images/Taelove7; p. 103 (5): Shutterstock Images/ Artiis; p. 103 (6): Shutterstock Images/Aerogondo2; p. 104-105 (B/G): Shutterstock Images/Alexander Vershinin; p. 116 (T): Getty Images/Javier Pierini; p. 117 (T): Shutterstock Images/Jktu_21; Back cover: Shutterstock Images/Vibrant Image Studio.

Front cover photography by Alamy/©Marc Hill.

The publishers are grateful to the following illustrators:

David Belmonte p. 44; Nigel Dobbyn p. 43, 49, 102; Q2A Media Services, Inc. p. 7, 55, 63, 118;
Jose Rubio p. 26, 119; Sean Tiffany p. 7.

All video stills by kind permission of:

Discovery Communications, LLC 2015: p. 2 (1, 3), 5, 10, 12 (1, 3, 4), 15, 20, 21, 22 (1, 3), 25, 30, 32 (1, 3, 4), 35, 40, 41, 42 (1, 3, 4), 45, 50, 51, 54 (1, 3), 57, 62, 64 (1, 3, 4), 67, 72, 73, 74 (1, 3), 77, 82, 84 (1, 3), 87, 92, 94 (1, 3, 4), 97, 102, 103, 116, 117, 118, 119, 120; Cambridge University Press: p. 2 (2), 8, 12 (2), 18, 22 (2), 28, 32 (2), 38, 42 (2), 48, 54 (2), 60, 64 (2), 70, 72 (2), 80, 84 (2), 90, 94 (2), 100.

Credits

The authors and publishers acknowledge the following sources of copyright material and are grateful for the permissions granted. While every effort has been made, it has not always been possible to identify the sources of all the material used, or to trace all copyright holders. If any omissions are brought to our notice, we will be happy to include the appropriate acknowledgements on reprinting.

p.3 (TL): Shutterstock Images/Sergiyn; p.5 (TR): Alamy/©The Photolibrary Wales/Steve Benbow; p. 10 (1): Getty Images/Steve Granitz/WireImage; p. 10 (2): Getty Images/Sonja Flemming/CBS; p. 10 (3): Alamy/©ZUMA Press; p. 10 (4): Getty Images/Steve MORT/AFP; p. 10 (5): Getty Images/Jasin Boland/NBC/NBCU Photo Bank; p. 10 (6): Getty Images/Alexander Tamargo; p. 10 (7): Alamy/©Jochen Tack; p. 10 (8): Alamy/©Pictorial Press Ltd; p. 10 (9): Alamy/©AF archive; p. 11 (TL): Alamy/©Blend Images/Jeff Greenough; p. 14 (CL): Shutterstock Images/FXQuadro; p. 18 (CL): Alamy/©Daniel Dempster Photography; p. 27 (TL): Alamy/©Everett Collection Inc; p. 33 (TR): Alamy/©Megapress; p. 37 (CR): Alamy/©Andreas Von Einsiedel; p. 39 (TL): Shutterstock Images/Julian Rovagnati; p. 47 (TL): Shutterstock Images/Ermolaev Alexander; p. 50 (1): Alamy/©MBI; p. 50 (2): Getty Images/Jupiterimages; p. 50 (3): Shutterstock Images/Michaeljung; p. 50 (4): Shutterstock Images/Pierdelune; p. 50 (5): Getty Images/MachineHeadz; p. 50 (6): Shutterstock Images/Denis Kukareko; p. 50 (7): Alamy/©Jim West; p. 50 (8): Shutterstock Images/oliveromg; p. 50 (9): Alamy/©age fotostock Spain, S.L.; p. 50 (10): Shutterstock Images/Sofia Andreevna; p. 51 (BL): Alamy/©Andres Rodriguez; p.53 (BL): Shutterstock Images/Mariyana M; p.53 (BC): Alamy/©Oote Boe 3; p. 56 (1): Shutterstock Images/Africa Studio; p. 56 (2): Shutterstock Images/Roadk; p. 56 (3): Shutterstock Images/Photosync; p. 56 (4): Shutterstock Images/Veronchick84; p. 56 (5): Shutterstock Images/Stephen Mcsweeny; p. 56 (6): Shutterstock Images/Africa Studio; p. 56 (7): Shutterstock Images/R.Legosyn; p. 56 (8): Shutterstock Images/Kellie L.Folkerts; p. 56 (9): Shutterstock Images/Liu Anlin; p. 56 (10): Shutterstock Images/MichaelJay Berlin; p. 56 (11): Getty Images/Wavebreak Media; p. 59 (CL): Shutterstock Images/PhotoSky; p. 63 (TR): Alamy/©Purcell Team; p. 64 (BL): Getty Images/Tim Hall; Back cover: Shutterstock Images/Vibrant Image Studio.

Front cover photograph by Alamy/©Marc Hill.

The publishers are grateful to the following illustrators:

Janet Allinger p. 6, 32, 54; Galia Bernstein p. 19, 25, 26, 31, 40, 41, 45, 55, 66 (TR), 67, 70; Anni Betts p. 2, 21, 28, 30, 60, 61, 68; Alberto de Hoyos p. 22 (1-5, 7, 9, 10), 58 (1-10); Nigel Dobbyn p. 4, 8, 48, 52 (TR), 62; Mark Duffin p. 44 (1-3, 5-7); Simon Ecob p. 9, 14, 15, 17, 24, 35; Q2A Media Services, Inc. p. 7, 19, 25, 26, 31, 40, 41, 44 (4), 45, 46, 52 (TL), 55, 65, 66, 67, 70; Jose Rubio p. 12, 13, 20, 22 (6, CR), 34, 42, 43, 58 (C); David Shephard p. 36; Norbert Sipos p. 38, 49.

All video stills by kind permission of Discovery Communications, LLC 2015.

Notes

Notes

Notes

Notes

Notes